PURPOSE, PASSION & PROFIT

To

From

I wish for you a life of wealth, health, and happiness; a life in which you give to yourself the gift of patience, the virtue of reason, the value of knowledge, and the influence of faith in your own ability to dream about and to achieve worthy rewards.

– Jim Rohn

Published by
Lessons From Network
www.LessonsFromNetwork.com

Distributed by
Lessons From Network
P.O. Box 93927
Southlake, TX 76092 817-379-2300
www.LessonsFromNetwork.com/books

ISBN-13: 978-0-9983125-6-9 (Paperback)

Printed in the United States of America.

PURPOSE, PASSION & PROFIT

Receive Special Bonuses When Buying
Purpose, Passion & Profit Book

To Receive, send an Email to
gifts@PurposePassionProfitBook.com

What Others Are Saying About
Purpose, Passion & Profit

"In Purpose, Passion & Profit, *long-time friend Kyle Wilson and his fellow contributors created a powerful book loaded with strategies, ideas, and inspiring stories and lessons that will help you achieve new levels of success.*"
– Brian Tracy, Author, Speaker, Consultant

"*It's time to rise and shine and fully express your talents, gifts, and abilities. Read, absorb, and drink deeply of the eclectic wisdom of this book, and do just that, now.*"
– Mark Victor Hansen, Co-Creator of World's Bestselling Book Series, *Chicken Soup for the Soul*

"Purpose, Passion & Profit *combine to make the north star leading us to a happy, fulfilled, and meaningful life. My friend Kyle Wilson weaves all three magically, and the result is a must read if you are ready to IGNITE!*"
– John Lee Dumas, Founder of the Award-Winning Podcast *Entrepreneurs on Fire*

"*I'm such a big believer in leading with your purpose and passion. Kyle and his fellow contributors share amazing examples of how to authentically lead with purpose and passion, in a way that allows profits to flow back. It is a must read!*"
– Lisa Haisha, Founder of The SoulBlazing™ Institute and Host of the Amazon TV show, *SoulBlazing with Lisa Haisha*

"*There is no better person to write a book called* Purpose, Passion & Profit. *My friend Kyle Wilson exemplifies and encompasses each of those terms. The other contributors share specific example of ideas and methods for doing so in your life both personally and professionally. It's a threefold recipe for a very next-level, legacy life!*"
– Bob Donnell, Founder of Everything Next Level

"*Kyle Wilson has done a wonderful job in bringing entrepreneurs, investors, business owners, and authors together to tell their stories. The Bible says "iron sharpens iron," and you will definitely be sharpened by reading the stories of these individuals in* Purpose, Passion & Profit.*"*
– Dave Zook, Author, Serial Entrepreneur, and Investment Strategist

"I know that there are no straight lines to success. Purpose, Passion & Profit not only shows you how to succeed, but also teaches you how to create a life of fulfillment."
– Todd Stottlemyre, Author of *Relentless Success*, Former MLB Pitcher and 3x World Champion

"In Purpose, Passion & Profit *the question of whether these three things can coexist is answered. Kyle Wilson and his amazing heart-centered group of authors not only show they can coexist, but they can also provide extraordinary success and, most of all, fulfillment. In a negative world, this beacon of light can help transform and inspire those that not only want a better life, but also want to make a difference in the world."*
– Reuben Salazar, Entrepreneur, Bestselling Co-Author, Business Coach

"My good friend Kyle Wilson knows how to create powerful books that inspire, motivate, and move you to become a better, more successful person. You owe it to yourself to benefit from all the great content he and his contributors passionately share to better your life!"
– Marco Santarelli Investor, Author, Host of the Top-Rated Passive Real Estate Investing Podcast

"There is no one better than Kyle Wilson to attract world-class thought leaders and reveal their most impactful wisdom! Kyle's friends are among the foremost influencers of business, personal development, and entertainment. Readers will cherish these compelling and significant stories for generations."
– Kelli Calabrese, #1 Bestselling Author of *Mom & Dadpreneurs*

"Part of success is preparation on purpose (Jim Rohn). Kyle Wilson's newest book Purpose, Passion & Profit *now provides 37 awe-inspiring, deeply personal stories of remarkable men and women! These amazing achievers have lived purpose-filled lives, pursuing passions across a broad range of endeavors including entrepreneurship, music, sports, business, leadership, and personal development. I encourage you to read this valuable book and then give it away to those who are on their journey of a purpose-filled life."*
– Tim Cole, 31-Year Marine Corps Colonel

"Every person who reaches some pinnacle of success in their life and work has that something special, that spark that spurs them into action no matter the odds. It is not about things that happen by chance, it is rather about the moment someone takes their chance. In each of these powerful stories there is a moment where the speaker stepped into their chance and made the world, our world, all the better for it. Purpose, Passion & Profit *can be summed up in one word: Powerful."*
– Kathi C. Laughman, CPC ELI-MP, Author – Speaker – Strategist – Certified Coach, Founder of The Mackenzie Circle LLC

"No one embodies purpose, passion and profit more than Kyle Wilson. Since I met him over 15 years ago I've watched him define a goal that would become his purpose and passion and execute it just about every single time. Not only has he been a genius at doing this for himself but for others."
– Ron White, 2 Time US Memory Champion, Speaker and Author

"Life and business have taught me that any meaningful achievement began and concluded with a compelling purpose—a why. Purpose, Passion, & Profit *echoes that ageless principle through modern-day triumphs and leaves the reader inspired to make a difference by discovering theirs."*
– Patrick Donohoe, CEO, Author, Podcaster

"I recommend this book to everyone who wants to improve their life through being their most authentic self, helping others, loving life, and making money while doing it."
– Michael Blank, Real Estate Investor, Teacher, Host of The Apartment Building Investor Podcast

"Take my highest recommendation and multiply it by ten and you have what I think about Kyle Wilson. The same can be said for this book. Kyle is a master, and those who work with him are professionals in the know."
– Chris Widener, Bestselling Author of *The Angel Inside*

"Success is when preparation meets opportunity and there is no better way to become prepared for a successful life then diving into Purpose, Passion and Profit. *My good friend and the longtime business partner of Jim Rohn, Kyle Wilson, has put together this powerhouse group who have collectively given you the essential tools you need to become valuable and successful in the marketplace allowing you to reach goals that you never thought possible."*
–Tommy Snyder, President 1691 Capital Partners

"'You are the average of the five people you spend the most time with' is one of Jim Rohn's most famous quotes and exactly describes the changes in my life after meeting his brilliant Biz Partner, Kyle Wilson, Dr. Tom Burns and other authors of Purpose, Passion & Profit. *These stories demonstrate that a big enough purpose breeds success—read them if you want to be unstoppable!"*
– Gary Pinkerton, Wealth Strategist, Navy Submarine Captain

"These amazing stories in this great book will give you the inspiration, motivation, and strategies to pursue your purpose and passion while making a profit. There is no better feeling than to be able to do that, and there is no better resource to inspire you. You'll savor these stories, and you'll want to share them with everyone you know."
– Monick Halm, Real Estate Investor and Founder of Real Estate Investor Goddesses

DISCLAIMER

The information in this book is not meant to replace the advice of a certified professional. Please consult a licensed advisor in matters relating to your personal and professional well being including your mental, emotional and physical health, finances, business, legal matters, family planning, education, and spiritual practices. The views and opinions expressed throughout this book are those of the authors and do not necessarily reflect the views or opinions of all the authors or position of any other agency, organization, employer, publisher, or company. Since we are critically-thinking human beings, the views of each of the authors are always subject to change or revision at any time. Please do not hold them or the publisher to them in perpetuity. Any references to past performance may not be be indicative of future results. No warranties or guarantees are expressed or implied by the publisher's choice to include any of the content in this volume.

If you choose to attempt any of the methods mentioned in this book, the authors and publisher advise you to take full responsibility for your safety and know your limits. The authors and publisher are not liable for any damages or negative consequences from any treatment, action, application, or preparation to any person reading or following the information in this book.

This book is a personal collaboration between a number of authors and their experiences, beliefs, opinions, and advice. The authors and publisher make no representations as to accuracy, completeness, correctness, suitability, or validity of any information in the book, and neither the publisher nor the individual authors shall be liable for any physical, psychological, emotional, financial, or commercial damages, including, but not limited to, special, incidental, consequential, or other damages to the readers of this book.

Additional Resources

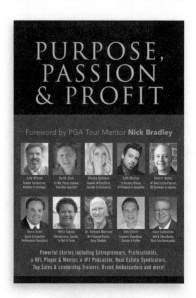

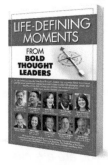

Order online www.LessonsFromNetwork.com/Books

Dedication

To the late Jim Rohn, Zig Ziglar, Charlie "Tremendous" Jones, Paul J Meyer, Og Mandino, Warren and Marge Wilson and other mentors that have shaped so many of us through their example and philosophy!

Acknowledgments

To Takara Sights, our editor and project manager extraordinaire, for your endless hours of work and passion in this book! Despite the complexities involved with a project like this you keep this a pleasure and always provide a first class result. A thousand praises! You are a rockstar! #millennialsrule

To Brian Tracy, Mark Victor Hansen, John Lee Dumas, Lisa Haisha, and all the amazing mentors and world class thought leaders who took the time to read this manuscript and give us their endorsements.

Foreword

by Nick Bradley

I have led a fortunate life.

By virtue of my vehicle, the great game of golf, I have taught famous actors, met presidents of the United States, and instructed players to number one in the world. I commentate to millions on TV and write bestselling instructional books.

Not bad for a kid who flunked high school back home in London.

What pulled me through, and drove me to the heights of success that I now enjoy, can be illuminated by this Jim Rohn quote:

> *"Formal education will make you a living. Self-education will make you a fortune."*

It was these kinds of quotes that elevated my thinking, leading me to believe that if I worked smart, became a value proposition, and invested in my personal growth, my goals would become realities.

Unfortunately, Jim isn't with us anymore, but Jim's secret weapon Kyle Wilson is.

I met Kyle Wilson five years ago at one of his mastermind group sessions. As a testament to the quality of that experience, some of the attendees in Dallas that week are still my friends today. Because Kyle is an expert in his craft, he has the uncanny ability to attract other experts who, like me, want to continue to grow into the best version of themselves they can. The mastermind events Kyle conducts are some of the best personal development seminars you can attend, period.

At the beginning of this introduction, I highlighted the unique people that golf has allowed me to meet. I didn't do this for bragging rights. I did it because Kyle Wilson is part of my inner circle, a valued person in my life, who I have so much respect for that I comfortably introduce him to the closest friends I value the most.

Purpose, Passion & Profit isn't just a flashy book title, and I will tell you why by sharing this short story.

At nineteen years old, I bought a book that Sir Nick Faldo, winner of six major championships had written. He was my golfing hero.

In the back of that book I wrote:

'"From this day onward, it is my duty to try and become the best."'

I signed that book and dated it 9.13.1989. I was nineteen years old.

Almost thirty years later in 2018, I met with Sir Nick at the Wells Fargo championship in Charlotte, North Carolina where I was TV commentating. In that meeting he did two things. First, he signed my book and wrote a cool message under the commitment I'd made to myself in 1989. Second, he asked me to work on his game as he prepared for the Seniors Open Championship played at St. Andrews in Scotland.

This story perfectly reflects the title of Kyle's new book *Purpose, Passion & Profit*.

My purpose was to be the best I could be.

My passion kept me going through the inevitable bumps in the road en route to success.

My profit was not only financial but also spiritual and professional.

Dreams, such as working with your hero on his golf game, can come true with the right formula in place. Success is only seen a fluke for people who have no plan to follow.

If you not only follow but actually live with the advice provided in Kyle's amazing book *Purpose, Passion & Profit*, you can and you will see your dreams become your reality.

Nick Bradley

Bestselling author of 7 Laws of the Golf Swing. *Works with some of the best players on the PGA & European Tour. International speaker and corporate trainer. https://www.nickbradleygolf.com/*

Table of Contents

"Let others lead small lives, but not you. Let others argue over small things, but not you. Let others cry over small hurts, but not you. Let others leave their future in someone else's hands, but not you."

– Jim Rohn

CHAPTER 1

On the Way Is Where You Find the Way

by Kyle Wilson

We had set up for people to fly into Dallas and Los Angeles for four days of filming. Conversations and interviews with Brian Tracy, Zig and Tom Ziglar, Mark Victor Hansen, Denis Waitley, John Maxwell, Les Brown, and dozens more of Jim Rohn's peers, colleagues, and friends were taking place, all in preparation for a tribute video I wanted to show Jim.

My mentor, friend, and business partner for 18 years, Jim Rohn, had been diagnosed with pulmonary fibrosis the year before. We had to cancel his last few appearances. He was getting worse.

We had so many amazing stories, testimonials, and sentiments of love from this amazing group of people. But I knew we were still missing one.

How could I put together this montage of amazing words of love and admiration from all these people in Jim's life and not have one of his main mentors, William E. Bailey?

Bill wasn't able to make the trip to Dallas or LA. He was in his 80s, had been sick, and said "Hey Kyle, I just can't make it. I will try to find a way to record and send in a video, although I'm not sure how I will be to do that."

I said, "Bill if you can't come to us, I will happily come to you."

A week later I flew into Lexington, Kentucky the night before we were to meet and rented a car. The next morning, I drove for a few hours east. Soon I was truly in the backwoods of Kentucky. I met Bill at his long-time family log cabin.

I had made it there and I planned to stay as long as Bill would have me. I had known Bill for many years. In fact, I'd published his *Rhythms of Life* book several years prior and had booked him on many of my stages. But to have a chance to spend time with this Horatio Alger winner, the founder of

Best Line Products, and again, one of Jim's true mentors was something I was honored to do.

After filming the tribute to Jim, Bill and I decided to go grab a late lunch.

I'll never forget that, when we were talking, he looked at me, and he said in a mentoring tone, "Kyle, you have a true genius about you. And your gifts have made room for themselves. There is no way you could've ever predicted meeting and working with Jim Rohn. How you arrived at what you do and your relationship with Jim is a byproduct of your calling and the hundreds and the thousands of things you did way before you ever met Jim. There's no way you could've ever predicted it."

Then after these almost prophetic words from Bill, we went back to our normal conversation.

Bill was right. I didn't even know who Jim Rohn was at age 27. There's no way I could have made it a goal of mine to get in the seminar business and eventually be the founder of Jim Rohn International, partnering and spending 18 years with this amazing man. That privilege was a product of hundreds of decisions prior to that.

Purpose

When people ask me what my purpose is, I always say, "My purpose comes from a desire to be my best, and a desire to be faithful with the opportunities in front of me."

I got into the seminar business serendipitously, and I believe I was guided there by always asking "How do I do my best at what is in front of me?" consistently through a series of opportunities and open doors as well as through challenges and often difficult circumstances.

Once in the seminar business, I had to learn how to successfully and consistently fill big rooms, which led to meeting Jim Rohn, Brian Tracy, Og Mandino, and many others, which then led to me making Jim an offer he couldn't refuse in 1993 to launch Jim Rohn International.

When people come to me saying, "Hey, I don't know my purpose," I always challenge them to simply take what's already in front of them and to be the best version of themselves.

One of my favorite quotes is from Napoleon Hill, "Never pray and ask for more, but always pray to do the best with what you already have."

I have found that philosophy to be foundational in what drives me. I'm always asking, "What's in front of me, and how do I be and make the best version of that?" which then oftentimes is what opens up doors for me that may have seemed totally disconnected from what I'm doing.

So many people ask me, "How did you meet and work with Jim Rohn, Brian Tracy, Darren Hardy, Mark Victor Hansen and Jack Canfield of *Chicken Soup for the Entrepreneur's Soul*, Zig Ziglar, Jeffrey Gitomer, rocker Phil Collen of Def Leppard, two-time Grammy winner Seth Mosley, or real estate investor and syndicator, Robert Helms, etc?" I have to say, in most cases, I never pursued any of them, the opportunities came to me as a byproduct of being a faithful steward over what I already had.

Of course, add to that working hard, being a student, making good decisions, thinking outside the box, surrounding myself with good people, having a win-win mindset, and finding ways to build platforms that bring value to other people.

Passion

When you are passionate, you then have the desire and reasons to get up early, stay up late, read the books, go to the seminars, make the calls, keep a journal, seek out mentors, and push through obstacles.

I love Jim Rohn's quote: "If you want to be successful, learn to bring value to the marketplace. If you want to be wealthy, learn to be valuable to valuable people."

Part of my passion is to deliver great value to the marketplace and to be valuable to valuable people.

This goes back to why I was so passionate about getting Jim's message out in the world through the products and events we created. We were able to impact millions of people. I still receive messages daily.

Today I am also passionate about not only finding and sharing my story and lessons, but also helping people find their own message, purpose, and passion.

In fact, a big part of why I wanted to do this book and share the many powerful stories in it is to inspire the reader to find their own purpose, passion, and profit!

Profit

Profit is the RESULT of bringing great value to the marketplace. You know something is good when it's profitable, most usually. And when you build a company and you have profits flowing in, that means you've found a way to serve a multitude of people in the marketplace.

I remember the last year before I sold my companies, not only me, but all 20 staff members and all the speakers I represented, including Jim Rohn, Dennis Waitley, Chris Widener, and Ron White, ALL experienced our most profitable year both as a company and individually. This meant we were bringing massive amounts of value to the marketplace. We built a team, we built a culture, and we built a vehicle that allowed not just Jim Rohn, not just me, but that allowed every single staff member, through profit sharing, to experience their most profitable year to date.

When you get your purpose and your passion in alignment, the profit will follow.

One of my favorite lines I preach often is, "We learn by doing."

You might not know where to begin. But once you get started, that will lead you to the next step.

I went from starting a car detail shop in a small town of 12,000 at age 19, to owning a service station at age 23, to getting into the seminar business at 28. I didn't know the seminar business, I had to learn it. But I learned by getting started and doing it. Then I had to learn to put on big events. Then how to be an agent. Then how to create products. I'd never created audio programs or DVD programs or books, but I had to learn to do that from the ground up. We went on to create hundreds of IP products and sell millions of books. Then came the internet. I had to learn to be an online marketer and create content, and I built over a million plus list. I had to learn to manage a team. Managing and leading a staff was one of the steepest learning curves I've ever undertaken. That required a lot of searching, a lot of seeking counsel. But I learned through trial and error. I then had to learn to sell a company and all that was involved. All these things I learned by doing. Too many times we think we already have to know it all when, in reality, there are some things you will never learn unless you just get started.

Ultimately, my purpose, passion, and profit revolve around my family and loved ones. Spending time both personally and professionally around people I'm aligned with philosophically and that I love and learn from drives me. I intentionally surround myself with people I am able to support and feel supported by and with whom I'm able to authentically be myself.

If I don't feel attracted to projects or the people I'm working with, it's really easy to say no.

Jim Rohn used to tell me, "Kyle, let's go stir the pot together and let's do something remarkable!"

I too, challenge you to tap into your purpose and passion and let the byproduct of profit lead you into a life of significance and making a difference!

You got this!

TWEETABLE

Profit is the RESULT of bringing great value to the marketplace. When you build a company and you have profits flowing in, that means you've found a way to serve the marketplace.

Kyle Wilson is a strategist, marketer, and entrepreneur. He leads the Kyle Wilson Inner Circle Mastermind and is the author of 52 Lessons I Learned from Jim Rohn and Other Great Legends I Promoted *and coauthor of* Chicken Soup For the Entrepreneur's Soul!

Kyle is founder of Jim Rohn International, YourSuccessStore, LessonsFromNetwork.com and KyleWilson.com. Kyle has filled big event rooms and produced 100s of programs including titles by Jim Rohn, Brian Tracy, Zig Ziglar, Denis Waitley, and recently the books The One Thing That Changes Everything, Life-Defining Moments from Bold Thought Leaders, Passionistas, The Little Black Book of Fitness, *and* Mom & Dadpreneurs. *Go to KyleWilson.com/connect to download Free books & audios and to connect on social media.*

CHAPTER 2

The Miraculous, Unstoppable You

From the NFL to Significance

by Keith Elias

I sat with my head down and my shoulders slumped. My soul felt heavy and weary like a pair of dirty, drenched socks. My head coach stood over me, and I don't recall his exact words (I'll explain why in a minute), but what I do remember is that as a result of his words my heart went into a panic. I knew this game was slipping away.

This was the biggest game of the season, Princeton versus Harvard, and while the world may have been more interested in a Notre Dame-Miami matchup, for us, this was like USA versus Russia in the '80 Olympics. And yes, Harvard is like Russia in this example, no matter what my friend from Harvard, Matt Birk, might say. It was late in the game, and though I felt we should have been a match for them, something awful happened. I am going to have to use a very bad word that starts with an "F."

I fumbled.

Seriously, I got hit on both sides, and it was one of those moments that all running backs can describe perfectly—as the ball slides out of your grasp, so does your hope, and an emptiness pervades your being because you have just let your team down. In no other place in life, except in marriage, have I ever felt such a profound responsibility to another. When I fumbled against Harvard in that game, I was gutted because I let my brothers down.

Harvard went on to recover the ball and score, and it was one of those moments in a contest when you feel your victory slipping away. It was one of those moments when life feels like it is going by too fast, and out of your control. And so I sat on the bench, head in hand, listening to my coach vomiting what must have been his fear, doubt, confusion, and panic over me—let's not forget, his livelihood was attached to my play and our win-loss record. But again, I don't remember exactly what he said, just how it felt, because in a split second something miraculous happened to me.

As the head coach departed, my position coach, Steve DiGregorio, ran up to me and said something that changed my life forever. First, he commanded me, "Hey, forget everything he just told you."

I looked up and nodded, "Yes, coach." And just like that, to this day I can't recall what my head coach said.

Then he grabbed my shoulder pads, lifted me up to meet his eyes, and said, "When you get back out there, you just be *you*, because when you're *you*, you're unstoppable." At that moment I felt a surge, a liquid lightning bolt, energize me, and new confidence birthed in my heart. The lion in the Tiger uniform returned.

On my very next run, I took the handoff going right, cut back to the middle of the field, broke three tackles—I was unstoppable—and bolted 56 yards for the back-breaking score. We never looked back and beat the Crimson on their home turf during the Head of the Charles weekend. That run was showcased the next week on *Good Morning America* as a birthday surprise for anchor Charles Gibson and probably had a hand in me getting invited to the NFL Scouting Combine and signing a contract with the New York Giants.

But don't get it twisted! The touchdown run isn't the climax of the story. It is merely the consequence of the climax. The revelation and understanding of the power of unleashing MYSELF to the universe, the power of finding my "YOU," is by far the greatest lesson from that day and the greatest miracle I can give to someone else. This lesson learned on the gridiron one Saturday afternoon in Boston served me well when I was forced to navigate one of the darkest times of my life.

I remember sharply what it was like to leave the NFL after six years of playing professionally—the loss of structure, the loss of finances, and the loss of identity. The loss. Truthfully, no matter how hard I told people football was what I did and not who I was, I found myself reeling at the prospect of re-identifying myself. I was a football player. I was known as a football player. I had always been a football player, until I wasn't. I was left with the inexorable question, *If I am a football player who no longer plays football, then who am I?* Where was my YOU?

I realize that feelings of loss and transition are not unique to the gridiron. Those who leave the military know the pangs of missing the esprit de corps. Many have experienced breakups, relationship betrayals, failed businesses, bankruptcies, loss of jobs, devastating health issues, and the death of loved ones, to name a few of the life events that can trigger the same feelings. Some players leave the game and experience a variety of these issues: loss of camaraderie and purpose, degrading health, and even discovering personal relationships that were founded more on what the player did than who he was. And we suffer a type of death. I know I did.

Not only did my career not measure up to my own expectations, but additionally, within a year I saw my relationship with my significant other dissolve before my eyes. It is difficult to talk about in a way that makes others understand.

My brother-in-law is a genius, prodigy concert pianist. We spoke one time about the transition many NFL and other professional athletes go through. I asked him to think of his own life. Since he was a child, he has been marked by this gift that set him apart. He had special tutors, went to special schools, and had a unique set of friends because of his gift.

Now, I told him, imagine at 30 years old, you're no longer allowed to play the piano ever again. You're no longer able to share that gift, no longer able to hang out with your special crowd, no longer able to make the money you used to make. Oh, and the woman you've been hanging out with for the last five years, she may or may not actually like you.

Recently, a former player and friend of mine, Ken Ruettgers, and I decided to write an allegory about what that transition is like—not just for players, but for all who, because of life's circumstances, have been forced to change direction and start over. We're calling it *When the Circus Leaves Town—How a Lion Learned to Hunt Again*. In it, our lion, Finley, has just learned that the circus has left him without him knowing about it.

It has been one of the easiest things for me to write because I was Finley. But, guess what, some of you have been Finley too. My circus was the NFL lifestyle. What's your circus? I've seen you walking around in the mall or on the bus like a zombie, your life feeling like your own personal coffin because he left you, because she died, because your dream turned into a nightmare, because of the hurt and betrayal—because life wasn't supposed to be this way.

So, what do we do?

We can quit, lay down and die, or submerge ourselves in the pleasures and slavery of drugs, sex, and other addictions. Or we can lament, blame others, grow bitter, and let our lives become the slow fade. Or...

Or...

Or, we can acknowledge the new reality, allow ourselves to grieve, cling to hope, muster courage, and begin the long climb back through self-discovery and into purpose and love again. When anyone becomes their "YOU," then they too become unstoppable. My true YOU isn't really about football at all. It's about rousing the spirit, quickening the heart, revealing truth, and awakening the YOU in others—to help them on their path of self-discovery and revelation. And that run against Harvard was just an expression of that truth. For me, it started with my reconnection to God. I found out that *I am* because of *who He is* and *what He has done*. That is my new identity, protected from all earthly assaults.

Now, in my work with our current and former NFL players and other men and women, I help them see their true YOU, so that they may see and understand their own ability to be unstoppable. I believe that if you don't quit in life, you can find what I did. Into the void left by broken relationships stepped new friends, my new tribe, and my captivating wife. Into the void of the game stepped purpose. Into the void of structure stepped adventure. Into the void of the circus stepped LIFE. Have you found your YOU?

Remember, there has only ever been one you, and you are truly, remarkably, and wonderfully made. So find you, and be you, then you too will be unstoppable.

TWEETABLE

Life can be painful. Don't quit. Into the void of broken relationships and lost opportunity can step new relationships, true purpose, and adventure. There has only ever been one you. You are truly, remarkably, and wonderfully made. Find you, be you, and you will be unstoppable.

After playing football at Princeton, Keith Elias left with 21 school and 4 NCAA records. He then played 6 years in the NFL with the Giants and Colts and became an international speaker. He now works for the NFL in Player Engagement, mentoring players through transition into and out of the game, coaching them in their purpose off the field. He is a mentor, speaker, and team builder who inspires and empowers others to find vision and purpose for their lives or companies. He truly believes, "When you become YOU, you are unstoppable." To contact for speaking, coaching, blog updates or just to connect, email keithelias@verizon.net.

CHAPTER 3

The One Question that Transformed My Relationships & My Business

by Meredith Bell

"I've learned that people will forget what you said, people will forget what you did, but people will never forget how you made them feel."

– Maya Angelou

Several years ago I belonged to GKIC (formerly Glazer-Kennedy Insiders Circle), a membership organization focused on helping entrepreneurs build their businesses. One morning, I started my day reading the latest issue of their newsletter, which was always packed with valuable marketing tips.

When I turned to page 12, I couldn't believe what I saw.

Staring at me from the page (and it covered a full page) was a copy of the hand-written thank you note I'd sent to then-President Bill Glazer and his team following the recent spring conference. I sat there dumbfounded for a moment, pondering the reason my letter was printed there. As I reflected, I recalled an earlier conference.

I had walked up to Bill and given him positive feedback about all the things I was enjoying at the event. His response surprised me: *"Thank you. You are such a positive person. You're always saying nice things to me. Can I get you to call me every day and tell me stuff like this?"*

Bill Glazer is a man who has achieved remarkable success in his career and his life. He's a millionaire many times over and has advised thousands of entrepreneurs. You wouldn't think he needs regular doses of positive feedback. But he does. We ALL do. As human beings, we have a desire to be validated and appreciated.

I believe his publishing my thank you note was a reaction to the way I apply my purpose and passion in my daily life. I'm committed to serving others so their life is enriched as a result of their encounter with me.

A little personal history to explain…

In my first career as an elementary school teacher, I got bored after a few years with the repetitive lessons. I then earned my masters degree and moved into a supervisory role at the school board office. I loved working with teachers to improve the way they interacted with their students. But I eventually discovered the position came with a price I wasn't willing to pay.

Over time, I experienced negative physical and emotional side effects as I tried to play politics and maneuver through the bureaucracy. I finally realized that I would never be able to thrive in that environment. It was time to make another shift, this time outside the field of education.

I decided to start my own consulting and training company. I would focus on helping people in the workplace learn to build strong, positive relationships with each other and with their customers.

But there were obstacles. I'd never taken a business course in college. I knew nothing about setting up and running a consulting company. I hadn't read a single book about marketing or selling.

What I did have going for me was belief in my desire to serve others and the confidence that I could learn what I needed to know. And along the way, I did.

My services included team building, leadership development, and customer service—areas where individuals must interact with each other to produce positive outcomes. I taught communication skills like listening, giving and receiving feedback, and resolving conflicts.

Over time, my purpose became clearer. I felt a passion bubble up every time I saw managers and employees learn how to have honest, open conversations and create better results. I received lots of referrals from clients due to the strong relationships I'd built.

Yet, it was lonely working by myself.

In 1990, I met Denny Coates, who also had a solo consulting practice. After a year of informal collaboration, we agreed that it made sense to merge our two companies, and we brought in a third partner at the same time. We added support staff along the way as we grew in response to the demand for our services.

Later, we realized that we wanted to expand our impact beyond the clients we served directly. In 1994 we made a decision to pivot from being a services firm to a software company. We developed a 360-feedback survey product, 20/20 Insight, which was customizable, economical, and easy to use. We were driven by a strong purpose to make a difference in the way people communicate at work.

We went on to create another program, Strong for Performance, to address a shortfall that plagues most training classes: the lack of follow-up and accountability to ensure people actually *use* their new skills back on the job. This tool provides practice, coaching, and feedback to help people make *lasting* improvements in the way they communicate and work together.

I've now worked with my two partners for nearly 30 years. We share a deep commitment to each other based on trust and respect. This bond has enabled us to survive and thrive despite the many challenges we've faced over the decades, including major downturns in the economy.

Many of our clients and resellers have done business with us for more than 20 years. They are like family to us. And part of the reason for that is, we aren't just interested in customer satisfaction. We want to build strong, long-term relationships.

During these past three decades, my own purpose has continued to evolve.

A single question in one book brought an essential aspect of my purpose into sharp focus.

The book was *The Prosperous Coach* by Steve Chandler and Rich Litvin, and the question leaped off the page at me:

"How can I serve this person so powerfully that they never forget our conversation for the rest of their life?"

It's rare that a single sentence can literally change your life, but that's what happened for me.

In that moment, I realized I wanted to engage in more conversations with impact. I spent considerable time trying to figure out: *What would it take to make a conversation so memorable that someone would remember it forever?*

I recognized one thing right away. It wasn't about waiting for my turn to talk about myself or the benefits of our products. I realized that serving others is something I already loved to do. I simply needed to take skills I already had, like listening and inquiring, to the next level.

I started repeating that question before every contact—whether it was making a phone call, appearing on a podcast, or giving a product demo. I was astonished at the responses I got from people who interacted with me. Their comments reinforced that I was onto something.

I further refined my purpose after listening to Episode 28 of the *10X Talk* podcast with Joe Polish, a world-renowned marketer, and Dan Sullivan, founder of Strategic Coach. Dan brilliantly gave a new twist to the meaning of APPRECIATE as it relates to *increasing in value*. We often associate this definition with THINGS that appreciate in value, such as stocks or real estate. But he extended the meaning to include PEOPLE.

When I focus on appreciating another person, I gain a fuller understanding of their value. I treat them differently because I'm focusing on the positives, and they pick up on this when we're together. They sense that I value them. As I bring my attitude of appreciation into the conversation, it boosts their feeling of self-worth. Their value increases in *their* minds as well as in mine.

I believe this partially explains why Bill Glazer responded the way he did to my positive verbal feedback and why my hand-written note ended up in their newsletter. My appreciation served to increase his feeling about his own value.

Another experience added a further dimension to my purpose: taking the VIA Survey for character strengths. My report helped me recognize and appreciate my #1 core strength, which is **LOVE**.

It took me a while to figure out how love applies in the context of business. For a variety of reasons, love isn't a word used regularly in the workplace. Then I connected the dots between love and serving. For me, loving someone means caring at a deep level about their well-being and being committed to supporting them on their life's journey. When I realized this, I crafted my purpose statement, which I write down each morning to remind me how I want to live my day:

> My purpose is to serve and love profoundly
> so others appreciate their own value and maximize it.

In my daily life, I make a conscious choice to be fully present with people I interact with so they feel they are the most important person in my world at that moment. I ask questions that show I'm genuinely interested in learning more about them. As I listen, I inquire about things that often no one else has ever asked them. I also offer observations or suggestions based on my own experiences.

What's NOT going through my mind: *What will I get out of this? How can I make a positive impression? When can I start talking about myself or our products?*

What IS going through my mind: *What can I contribute that would be beneficial to them?*

Throughout the conversation, I strive to sense what they aspire to have, be, or do; and I find a way to express their value.

For instance, I talked with a woman who worked full-time and was starting her own consulting business on the side. Though she was a skilled workshop facilitator and executive coach, she'd temporarily lost perspective about her capabilities and was filled with self-doubt. Here are excerpts from two notes she sent me.

Day of the conversation…

"Thank you again for investing your time, your wisdom, and your heart today. I feel as if I have inhaled truth, and I can feel myself re-framing."

Two months later…

"I have been thinking about you a great deal lately. You'll never know how much mileage our one conversation has provided me."

I get up every day feeling a deep passion and enthusiasm for my work. I ask myself, *"Who can I serve today?"* Sometimes, the answer is ME because I need to take care of myself. Most often, it's the people I've scheduled appointments with. When I'm out and about, it could be the cashier at the grocery store or the server in a restaurant.

What can I do to enrich the life of the person who's in front of me right now?

The profit we achieve in our business comes as a result of living my purpose and passion. At the end of many conversations—and with no prompting from me—the other person frequently wants to know more about our products. In the process of sharing that information, we often discover our solutions are an excellent fit for a problem they've been struggling with.

At that point, there's a natural opportunity to talk about how our assessment and development tools can help them increase their return on investment in their training programs. I love being able to share success stories that illustrate the positive impact our software has had on others.

Because I've been an entrepreneur for more than 35 years now, family members and friends sometimes ask me if I ever think about retiring. I always have the same response: NO!

I have a deep desire and personal responsibility to impact as many lives as possible during my lifetime. There are still so many who don't know how to communicate in a way that creates trust, respect, and loyalty. There are more transformations waiting to happen, and I'm having too much fun living out my purpose and passion to stop.

TWEETABLE

Focus on serving others profoundly, through intense listening and thoughtful questions. They're likely to remember you and the conversation for the rest of their life.

Meredith Bell is the co-founder and president of Performance Support Systems, a global software company. Their award-winning tools help leadership coaches and human resources/training professionals get a positive ROI on their learning and development programs. Meredith is a strong relationship-builder, and many clients have done business with her company for more than 20 years. Download your free ebook and connect on social media at:

https://meredithbell.me/

meredith@StrongForPerformance.com

CHAPTER 4

A Word to the Wi$e

by Jeff Huston

As a Midwest farm kid, I grew up with words like net worth and equity, and so I've always had a positive view of financial success. I was taught to value and respect people who achieved a high level of success with their money, and so, even from a young age, I wanted to be successful. Unfortunately, I wasn't very good in school. My report card usually showed C's and D's. I barely graduated from high school (let alone college).

I married my high school sweetheart at age 18, and we came back to work the family farm in 1980. My timing was off though, and within three years, we found ourselves in the middle of a full-blown depression in the farm economy. I remember telling my wife one day that "the light at the end of the tunnel had been temporarily turned off." I eventually had a personal auction, and the proceeds allowed me to pay down debt enough so I could hang onto the farmland, but in the process, I lost my occupation. So, I found myself with a wife and two kids, no college education, and no real prospects for building the life I had imagined.

I took a job working in a factory. I was making $15,000 per year. A little piece of me died every day I went into that job. I wanted more but didn't see a path of how that could happen. During that time, I was introduced to someone who would eventually become a key mentor of mine. He told me, "Jeff, a man is worth about $8 per hour from the neck down...from the neck up, it's unlimited. Going forward, you need to decide which end you're going to earn your income with." That advice helped me see the value of being a life-long learner. Not a single year has gone by since then that I have not been involved in a coaching program of some sort.

One day, a friend of mine called me up and said, "Jeff, I saw something the other day, and when I saw it, I thought of you. I think you'd be great at it." That comment introduced me to the world of financial services. I left my factory job, and I spent the next 25 years building a business of helping people with their finances. I built a boutique firm that helped thousands of clients achieve a greater level of financial independence and security until I sold the firm in 2010. Zig Ziglar use to say, "You will get all you want in life, if you help enough other people get what they want." I experienced that to be true. My firm helped a lot of clients, and in the process, I was financially rewarded. There were years when my income tax bill was seven figures. I was incredibly humbled and grateful for what was happening. Even though I was working hard, I still found my success hard to believe.

As people heard about what our firm was doing, I started getting asked to speak at conferences and events, and eventually, I opened a branch office in Los Angeles. That decision started a chain of events that led me to discover a lesson worth more than money.

I was flying every other week from Minneapolis to LA. One Thursday evening, I was flying home from John Wayne Airport. I had gotten an upgrade, so I was in first class. Sitting next to me was an older gentleman who was well dressed and who seemed like he had things all together. I didn't engage in conversation with him until we were descending into Minneapolis. I took off my headset and said something to him, and we chatted for a bit. In the process, he told me that it was his 92nd birthday. After I congratulated him, I paused and said, "Let me ask you a question. What advice would a seasoned life veteran, such as yourself, have for a young buck who's in the middle of fighting the battles of life and business?" He thought for a moment, then said, "I lived most of my life 15 minutes ahead." Then he went quiet and went back to looking out the window.

I said, "I don't understand, what do you mean?"

He looked back to me and said, "Well, when I was driving into work in the morning, I was thinking about what I had to do when I got there. When I went to lunch with someone, I would think about what I had to do when I got back to the office. And when I would go to one of my son's ball games, I found myself thinking about what I needed to do when I got home...."

He finished by commenting, "I lived my life 15 minutes ahead....If I could do it all over again, I'd be more present in the moment."

I was blown away by his words. I was 46 years old at the time, and I knew I was exactly like him. I was living my life 15 minutes ahead. I was accomplishing a lot, but I realized I was way better at "doing" than I was at "being."

I spent the next few months thinking about my conversation with him. I never knew his name, and I never saw his face again, but his message to me was inescapable. I knew I wanted to change. I knew I didn't want to keep living my life 15 minutes ahead. I knew I wanted to be more present. But how does a person break such an ingrained habit?

A few months later, I was checking in at a pro shop for a round of golf when I noticed a jar of ball marker chips (they look like poker chips, but they have the logo of the golf course on them). As I stood there waiting for them to process my transaction, I had the idea to buy one and start carrying it in my pocket as a reminder for me to "be present." Ten years have passed, and I still carry one. Every day! I keep it in my change pocket, and it helps me to remember to slow down. I call it my gratitude chip because I've discovered that a grateful mindset helps me to stay present.

Let's say I'm in the drive-thru at a coffee shop. I'm behind someone, and the wait is longer than I want it to be. So, I reach in my pocket to get the exact change. That way, I can do the transaction as quickly as possible when it's my turn...but when I see the chip, it reminds me, "Jeff, slow down and be present in this moment...don't run 15 minutes ahead!"

After 10 years of carrying my gratitude chip, I'd like to tell you I'm 100% present all the time, but most days I'm still a knucklehead. But, I'm less of a knucklehead than I used to be!

A few years ago, I designed and manufactured my own gratitude chip. On one side it says, "Be Present." On the other side it says, "Be Grateful." I'd be happy to send you one.

In 2010, after selling my financial services firm, I started investing in real estate with my son-in-law. We specialize in providing "affordable housing for modest income people." My son-in-law manages the rental and operations side of the business, and I work to find investors who are looking to grow their wealth without Wall Street risk.

The gratitude chip continues to impact the way we do business every day. We start every meeting with what we call "Going BIG." BIG is an acronym. It stands for "begin in gratitude." When we have a staff meeting, or any other kind of meeting, we always ask everyone present to share one thing they are grateful for. It could be something significant, or it might be something small, but setting the example that gratitude is a core value of ours has helped our business to grow 10X in the last five years.

Today my work is focused in two areas:

3D Money is our private equity firm that looks for investors interested in growing their money through real estate. We help people create financial certainty in uncertain times.

3D Money Guy is an extensive collection of resources and a website dedicated to coaching and inspiring others on their financial journey.

I believe that the superpower of the 21st century is gratitude because I've found that nurturing a culture of gratitude and being present sets our business apart. Our tenants, employees, vendors, contractors, and investors all know what we stand for, and in this upside-down world, it has been a game changer for us to take a stand on what we value instead of just trying to blend in like everyone else.

Presently Grateful,
Jeff Huston

TWEETABLE

The past is good; the future is good, but people who live in the present are the happiest and the ones who get the most accomplished.

Jeff Huston is a real estate investor and the creator of 3D Money, a private equity firm that helps investors grow their money outside of Wall Street risk by investing in cash flow real estate. 3D Money helps investors create certainty in uncertain times. Jeff is also the creator behind 3D Money Guy, an extensive collection of resources and website dedicated to coaching and inspiring others on their financial journey. If you would like to receive a free Gratitude Chip, go to www.3dmoneyguy.com and click on "Gratitude Chip."

CHAPTER 5

From My Parent's Basement to Two Grammys

by Seth Mosley

grew up in a small town called Circleville, Ohio. You've never heard of it. It is a small dot on a map 40 miles south of Columbus. And it's claim to fame is not music. It's...wait for it...

PUMPKINS! Our town is so proud of their pumpkins that they even built a water tower that looks like a pumpkin and hosts a week long pumpkin extravaganza every year called The Pumpkin Show. Heck, my parents were so proud of it, they even entered me in the pumpkin baby parade! So I hope you're getting the point that I wasn't born in Music City, USA.

My first exposure to music was in church. When I couldn't even walk yet, my parents would take me to their choir rehearsals and let me sit on their lap, and I'd memorize all of the songs before I could put sentences together. As I grew up, my dad (who wasn't really all that musical) would take me to concerts and buy me CDs. My first CD was from a band called Newsboys. You'll find out later why this is worth noting. Music was a constant part of my development, and I started to learn piano and guitar, probably having a total of about five lessons, but teaching myself instead. I eventually started leading on stage at church when I got into my teenage years. The only reason I ended up on stage was because there was no one else. I helped out with my youth group a ton, saw a need, had a passion, and raised my hand. I had never actually sang in front of anyone before, and being on stage was actually quite nerve-racking. But it was the way I felt like I could serve.

Eventually, I figured out a way to start recording myself and my really bad songs on my parents' computer at home. I eventually saved up enough money to buy some basic gear and start a recording studio in our basement. I was HOOKED. I would only come up for air, food, and water. And that was where I found my calling as a music producer and songwriter. I learned the art of this creative process by doing it over and over again, really badly, I might add. Then, one day I finished a song that I felt like wasn't totally embarrassing and uploaded it to the internet. I put my work out there. And I got lots of good feedback from people. I thought maybe I was onto something. And then I did something crazy that would change my life forever.

I had a friend named Mike. He was way cooler than me. He had a band. He played guitar really well. I called him up one day and said, "Hey Mike, guess what? I'm a music producer now and I have this sweet studio," which in reality was a computer and a couple speakers and a few microphones, and it was crazy for me to call myself a music producer. "I want to produce your band's record. And I'll do it for 100 bucks!"

"Ummm...sounds good," he answered.

Profound conversation, I know. Doesn't sound life-changing, I know. But let me tell you why it was.

I produced their five song EP, spent countless days and months slaving away over every detail of the sound. And by the way, I didn't know what I was doing. I had never done this before with anyone else's music. So I was learning how to actually produce as we went. When we all finally decided it was great, we put it out there. And it was a hit. At least two dozen copies sold. But then, my phone rang one day, and I remember exactly where I was sitting, in my dad's office at home. I picked up, "Hello?"

"Hi, my name is Carl, and I have a recording studio up in Columbus. I heard this record you did. You are doing some great stuff." It took me a minute to figure out, "Does he have the wrong number? Oh, THAT record that we just did in my parents' basement!"

"I'm expanding my production business and need someone to take over creative," he said. "Would you like to come and work for me and produce full-time?"

Meanwhile, on the other end of the line, I was internally freaking out. I was enrolled to go to college for music business, probably to learn how to be a producer anyway, and here this guy was offering me a full-time job to start doing it RIGHT AWAY!

So, like any smart person, I said yes and started working two weeks later. I was doing the job that I was going to go to college to hopefully get. And I was getting paid for it! I would have paid the guy for the experience, let alone make a full-time salary. And working for him was where I got my 10,000 hours. I didn't care what I was doing. Some days I was producing bands and other days I was learning how to solder headphone cables together. It was all a blast! I was just pumped to be in the environment, and the best thing I could do was to serve any way possible. I learned 10 times more by going in saying, "How can I serve?" rather than "How can I impress someone?"

This was a whirlwind year and a half. I loved it but had an itch inside to do my own thing. So I started my own band, trying to be as cool as my friend, Mike! And like anything else I do in life, I threw myself into it completely. I set up something like a telemarketing center, again in my parents' basement, and we made 50-100 phone calls a day offering to come and play at different venues across the country. Most people said no. But if we got one yes for the day, you'd better believe we were doing backflips! We ended up filling up a whole tour and then 150 shows for three solid years. We even ended up going all the way across the ocean to Sweden and played my favorite show in my entire touring career. Why? Because it was at that show that I met my wife.

We instantly knew. There was no question in my mind. She had never been to our country, and didn't even have a passport. But this didn't matter because it was meant to be. We got married exactly a year later and got our first house together in Nashville, TN—Music City, USA.

I should mention that I never made any money at the band. I was producing records for artists on the side to keep the band afloat. It eventually got to be so much of a burden because I was trying to be three things at once—a husband, a songwriter, and an artist. I learned the hard way from this season: IF YOU CHASE TWO RABBITS, YOU CATCH NEITHER. I was lacking the one key thing I needed to achieve success at any of them, FOCUS.

F - FIERCE

O - OBSESSIVE

C - CONCENTRATED

U - UNRELENTING

S - SACRIFICE

You probably know by now which path I chose. I took off the artist hat and decided to spend all my time at home becoming the best music producer and songwriter that I could be. I started a company called Full Circle Music because of this.

Remember how I told you my first CD I got when I was a kid was Newsboys? Well, the first major label project I was hired to produce in Nashville was, you guessed it—Newsboys. It was a record called *Born Again*. Talk about a full circle moment. I wore their records out as a kid growing up, and here

I was getting to press record and help bring to life a record for this same band that I loved so much. Mind you, I had never produced a label project before. I felt like I was still winging it. But the one thing I knew how to do was to serve. So I looked for any way to do that possible. Sometimes that meant producing their music, and sometimes that meant driving them in a car downtown to Atlanta and back for a meeting. Just like my time in the studio in Columbus, it didn't matter what I was doing. I was just immersed in music and loving every second.

Needless to say, the sky has been the limit for Full Circle Music since then. We have won two Grammy Awards, four Dove Awards, Billboard's #1 Producer of the Year in 2013, and SESAC #1 Songwriter of the Year in 2014. We have had 22 #1 radio singles and been a part of countless Gold and Platinum records sold worldwide. Our songs have been in major Hollywood films and TV commercials. And guess what our number one company core value is? SERVANTHOOD.

My hope is that my story and my success can remind you that if I can do it, anyone can do it. I was not born in LA or Nashville. I didn't come from a musically successful family. I barely have any formal music training. I have no college degree. And I saw my first #1 when I was 22, and I'm 30 now, so it really isn't even about age.

It isn't even about who is the most trained, qualified, or resourced. It is about who has the most drive, passion, and stick-to-it-iveness. But most of all, it is about being a servant. None of my success in life has been because I am the most gifted person in the room. In fact, it's been the opposite. I've had to serve, because I've been in over my head every season of my life. I've been in rooms and sat at tables I didn't deserve to sit at; I hadn't earned any right to. But what goes a lot further than trying to be impressive, is to look at who is sitting across from you in the room and asking, "How can I serve this person right now?" Sometimes for me, it has nothing to do with music. But that's ok. Because at the end of the day, music is what I do. It isn't who I am. Who I am is a servant. And though it sounds completely counter-intuitive, being a servant brings the greatest satisfaction out of anything you can do in life. Money gets old and goes away. Cars lose their novelty. Exotic vacations get boring. #1s fall off the chart. But serving others, now that's something that we all have deeply ingrained in us as humans. Becoming a servant is the highest thing in life we can achieve.

This idea of servanthood is what inspired me to start Full Circle Academy. We are on a mission to change the music industry from the inside out, by finding and empowering the next generation of producers, songwriters, and artists to make music at the highest possible level. If we have anything to do with it, this next generation won't be famous because they are rock stars, but they will be famous because they are serving this world like it has never been served before. Music has power. It changes lives, and even saves them sometimes. We want to be a part of speaking life into anyone trying to make it in the music business, and to give them a place to learn how. Full Circle Academy is doing this by providing education and mentorship through real-world hands-on experience and virtual coaching.

As a husband and a father of two beautiful daughters, I am especially blessed to have a world-class recording studio in our house. People come to me. I get to spend time with my family starting in the morning and as soon as sessions are finished. I'm intentional to put my family and spiritual life first.

I'm honored to share my story in this book. I never dreamed I would have a platform to share my philosophy and ideas outside the music world. In fact, in 2016 Kyle Wilson pushed me way outside my comfort zone when he ask me to speak and share my story at his 3-day Weekend Event with Brian Tracy, Darren Hardy, and other professional speakers.

I've learned to always answer the calls from your mentors and the people in your life with a *yes*. Good things are always on the other side.

TWEETABLE

It sounds completely counter-intuitive, but becoming a servant is the highest thing in life we can achieve. #fullcirclemusic

Seth Mosley, at only the age of 30, is a two-time GRAMMY award winning producer, the 2013 Billboard Magazine #1 Christian Music Producer of the Year and #3 Christian Songwriter, 2014 SESAC Christian Songwriter of the Year, and the writer of 28 charting radio singles. Seth has written over 700 songs. Seth's recent production credits include: High Valley, Michael W. Smith, TobyMac, for KING & COUNTRY, Unspoken, Jeremy Camp, Sidewalk Prophets, Audio Adrenaline, Blanca, Moriah Peters, and Jared Anderson. Seth Mosley is the Founder of Full Circle Music www.fullcirclemusic.org | info@fullcirclemusic.org Instagram: thesethmosley

CHAPTER 6

Listening to Those Who Made a Difference

by Willa Gipson

I was born in 1963. Although my dad was a good man, he didn't uphold his financial obligation to our family. As a result, my mom divorced him when I was six years old. From that day forward, my mom showed me what hard work and hustle would do in life.

She worked two jobs to make sure I had everything I needed and most of what I wanted. She sacrificed and paid for a Catholic school education for five years so that I could get a good educational foundation. The neighborhood school, in her opinion, was not sufficient for my early years of education.

Mom exposed me to ballet and acting lessons, neither of which I was really interested in. When I was attending Our Mother of Mercy Catholic School, I badly wanted to play basketball, but Momma was apprehensive because she didn't want me to get hurt. It took the persuasion of Coaches Ezell and Ethel Woolridge coming to our house to convince Momma to let me play. I am so thankful for the Woolridges. It was at that point that athletics became my passion.

Momma built the first brick house in our neighborhood of Stop Six in Fort Worth, TX with nothing but her hard work and sheer determination. Although our home was broken into and vandalized a dozen times which greatly scared us, we survived, just Momma and me.

I skipped the sixth grade in Catholic school because of a test on which I scored a high grade. I continued to perform well, and I was ready to enter high school very early. My momma didn't listen to the naysayers who said I was too young to attend high school at the tender age of 12 and who suggested that she instead should hold me back a grade or two. Instead, she listened to herself which inherently allowed me to listen to my own abilities with confidence. I went to high school, and thank God, I had a mentor and high school coach, Marti Powell, who saw potential in me and developed some of the raw athletic talent I had. She nurtured me as a 12-year-old freshman and instilled within me additional confidence. My village was encouraging and didn't try to hold me back. Along the way, my high school coach helped me see that I could achieve as a high school student-athlete despite my age.

When I was ready to go to college, my village grew, and once again, Momma didn't listen to the negative comments about me being devoured in the college scene at age 16. Because I had some athletic talent, God placed into my life head volleyball coach, Sinah Goode, who invited me to play college volleyball at Texas Wesleyan College. She gave that 16-year-old from a low-income neighborhood a chance to pursue her dream of playing collegiate volleyball. She didn't think I was too young. Furthermore, she believed in me, and I soaked up all of her mentorship. I didn't know we were low income because I had everything I needed and much of what I wanted, but that was the case. Sinah even took an interest in me and taught me how to waterski. Ha, I had never even been to a lake. I am so thankful today for Sinah Goode, my freshman year coach. Becky Hughes, who I truly appreciate, became my college coach for the remainder of my three years. In fact, it was Becky Hughes who nominated me for induction into the National Association for Intercollegiate Athletics Hall of Fame. Proudly, I was inducted into the class of 1991. I truly listened to my high school and college coaches because they felt the need to help me grow and develop as a young, aspiring athlete.

I graduated from college at the age of 19 and was ready to enter the workforce. Because my mom taught me that I could do anything in life and not to listen to the dream crashers, I entered the teaching and coaching profession at a high school with confidence when I was just 20 years old. Today, I credit my mom with my desire and determination to succeed. She was the pure, non-pretentious example and inspiration in my life. I thank God that I was able to move my mom away from a neighborhood that began to deteriorate, but I am thankful for being a product of that neighborhood where I was reared with godly principles by a phenomenal woman.

Five years into my teaching and coaching career, I pursued a postgraduate degree so that I could position myself to become an education administrator. After receiving the degree, I became an assistant athletic director, then a high school assistant principal. I finished my last 17 years on this path as a director of athletics overseeing three high schools and seven middle schools.

Along the way, I was inducted into three Halls of Fame for my time as an all-American athlete and athletic administrator. In my 22nd year as an educator, my dear friend who was a high school principal at the time approached me about a network marketing opportunity. I had dabbled in another network marketing business for eight months but was more interested in my career than in the opportunity at the time. This time, when Susan approached me, I was ready to take a look at what could potentially create some extra income for my family and me and what could ideally allow me to retire early. When I saw what Susan wanted to share with me, I made the decision that day to commit to building a residual income with a vehicle that was not product based. You see, I made the decision to listen to someone of credibility and influence.

In spite of working 70-80 hours a week as an athletic director, being a mom and fulfilling my church obligations, I found a couple of hours per week to work my business. I had to develop the mindset that I was now a business owner, and if I wanted my business to be successful, I had to be fully committed and leave no excuses for a lack of success. Today, I have nearly 20,000 people on my team across the country, and because of what they have done, I am the #27 income earner in my business out of hundreds of thousands of independent associates. My ongoing goal is to help as many people as I can achieve freedom of time and finances.

Because I made a decision to enhance my life, I was able to retire from my position in education at the age of 49. I now control my life without someone else controlling it.

Over my 55 years of living, I have learned several things about myself. Most important is, when I make up my mind to engage in something, I put my full effort into reaching the goal. Whether it's a relationship, multiple school degrees, or success in business, I am focused on the end result I seek. Second, I remove negative people from my life. I choose who I allow to be in my life. I believe it is an intrinsic choice to be happy or unhappy. I control my happiness, and I want to be around others who control their happiness. Third, I have learned over the years that I can do all things through Christ who strengthens me.

My purpose for sharing my story in this incredible book is to reach someone like me who is pondering how to get ahead in life and flourish in spite of his or her environment. I strongly believe that we have choices to make in our lives, whether we were born in the richest of families or in the most poverty-stricken neighborhoods. I am proud of who I am and where I came from, but I chose to be more and to have more. My momma instilled within me that strong work ethic to go get what I wanted. Because I made a decision to be more and have more, and by the grace of God, today I have built my dream home, have become a residual millionaire, and have earned free vehicles from my company along the way. I am a three-time Hall of Famer as well as an all-American athlete. My mission is to help as many people who are willing to enjoy life like I have because there is a better way for those who are willing to get it. Daily, I instill in my own kids, my pride and joys Whitney and Wesley, that they too can do more and have more with a little willpower and determination.

I chose not to listen to the negative voices that did not have the passion or drive to become someone better. I truly believe the best is yet to come, and I will continue to reach for higher heights. That is my passion.

As you have read through this brief chapter, I trust you will ask yourself the question, "Who am I listening to regarding the dreams and goals for my life?" We all have close friends and family whose opinions we value, but no one knows the desires of your heart better than you. When people thought I was nuts for making the decision to engage in network marketing while working a full-time job and raising a family, I chose to remember why I started my business.

Listen to the people who have what you want and those who have their arrows aligned in the same direction you want to go. In your own unique way, seek to emulate their style and approach, adding your own personal touch. Surround yourself with positive people and run from those who articulate the negative thoughts that can tear down your spirit and discourage you.

Listen to those who fill your soul with the confirmation of Philippians 4:13: *I can do all things through Christ who strengthens me.*

TWEETABLE

I had to develop the mindset that I was a business owner. If I wanted my business to be successful, I had to leave no excuse for a lack of success. I choose who I allow in my life that will enhance it. Choose wisely to whom you listen.

30-year educator Willa Gipson has been a teacher, coach, assistant athletic director, assistant principal, and director of athletics. She has been inducted into three Halls of Fame for athletics. Her Stream Energy network marketing business of 13 years has elevated her to the position of the #27 income earner of hundreds of thousands in the company. Today, Willa actively helps others who seek time and financial freedom. When Willa is not working her network marketing business, she is on the golf course or in her boat with family and friends. Willa is the proud mom of Whitney, 27 and Wesley, 25.

Email: weezah44@yahoo.com

CHAPTER 7

But, What If You Could?

Generosity, The Ultimate Investment

by Jerry Horst

"Live this life as though it were your last."

– Robert Helms

Every person is born with purpose and destiny, along with all of the gifts and equipment needed to fulfill that destiny. That seemed obvious to me as far back as I can remember. Life was exciting with the pursuit of endless possibilities and the expectation that anything was possible. I had this sense that life was an immeasurable gift, that there was a purpose to be discovered, a mystery and an adventure of immense value and reward to be unraveled.

Children are born optimists, but the disappointments and pressures of life tend to erode the sense that anything is possible…. But what if it didn't? It's an interesting question, isn't it?

Although we grew up not lacking any ordinary needs, the idea of wealth was not a concept central to our family or upbringing, except in my mind. For reasons unknown to me, I always expected that I would be very rich, and in my mind, that looked like having abundance to bless everyone around me. Somehow the ability to bring joy and value to others felt right, very fulfilling, even powerful.

I have observed that some of the wealthiest people I have known have treated even their table servers with the highest honor, which leads me to a deep belief that true wealth is seen in what you give, in respect, in honor, and even in money. My eyes opened to a much bigger picture of wealth and relational generosity, which has impacted my life profoundly.

There's a common thought that one should be satisfied with enough to meet basic personal needs, and anything beyond that is sometimes considered materialism or greed. But what if it isn't? There is a verse in the Bible that says each person should work so that he has an abundance to give to those in need, and that seemed like a higher, more intelligent thought to me. A friend once told me, "God created giving for the giver of it, not for the receiver. So that you would know how it feels to be just like Him."

Like most young boys of that era, I delivered papers, mowed lawns, and did anything else I could to earn a few bucks. I had this sense that as soon as I was old enough to drive, I would be able to do almost anything! So when I got my license, I took two jobs and started a side business.

My first construction job required leaving at about 5:30 am and arriving back home at about 6:30 pm, just in time to make it to the drive-in pizza joint, where I was the night manager. As the manager, I was the last one out the door after everything was cleaned for the next day, which typically happened around 12:30 am. Fortunately, being 16 meant I had even enough energy to start a side business doing some commercial lawn mowing. What a summer that was! I was able to buy my first car for $1,500, give $2,000 to some local charities that I was enthused about, and I still had something left in the bank. I felt like a king!

In 1975, a couple of years after that great summer, I walked into a bank, asked to see the president, and after some small talk, explained that I wanted to start my own construction company and would need a line of credit to fund my business aspirations. I was 18 and literally expected that he would most likely fall off the back of his chair laughing. Imagine my complete shock when he replied by saying, "The bank will be honored to be a part of your success story. Federal law requires us not to release any funds for three days; come back then, and we will have processed all the paperwork."

I remember walking out of the bank thinking, "What just happened? How was that even possible?"

A few years later, when I met my wife, Sue, our lifestyle expectations were rather simple, mostly because we just didn't know a lot of people of extraordinary wealth, and neither of us grew up in abundance by today's standards. Consequently, we often had more money than we needed or planned for, and we discovered the joy of giving and how easy and delightful it was to be able to "change the world," even if it was only a very small part of the world.

Twenty years later, in one of the most unplanned, serendipitous events, I was able to buy a commercial construction company which enabled us to give more in that first year than we had ever made in any previous year!

There were times in our lives when we literally had millions in the bank…and then there was this other time.

Like many in our business of real estate development and construction, 2008 was a game changer, one that lasted for many years! Year after year, we were faced with the option of building and selling new homes, each one at a loss, in order to pay the debt on our inventory of building lots. The alternative would have been to accept and declare our insolvency immediately, which seemed like a sudden drop off a financial cliff. While we never fell short on any financial obligation, the bank regulators were telling our bank that they had to call our loans because "Nobody continues to make payments, while losing so much money year after year." Thankfully, because of a thirty-year history with our bank, they never did call any of our loans, even though our accountants assured us that it would be unrealistic to expect that the bank would not call all of our loans within the year.

This was new territory for me. After thirty-five years of extraordinary success, abundance, and prosperity, facing impending loss for what seemed like a very long time, was devastating.

They say that wealth rarely passes successfully to the next generation. But what if it can? What if there are a lot of things "they say," which are invitations to prove otherwise? Of course, creating wealth involves an entirely different gift set and mindset than inheriting it. But what if it was possible to prepare children not to manage but to exponentially build wealth on the foundation that you have laid?

Near the beginning of this season of unprecedented loss, our two oldest sons had just returned home from college. Instead of pursuing their intended careers, they both chose to throw themselves into turning around the family business, which I don't think they had ever seriously thought about becoming part of until that time. Our oldest daughter had already worked with me for nearly a decade. Fighting a prolonged battle together has a way of deeply connecting people in a way little else can.

In the midst of what seemed like certain financial doom—the loss of a lifetime's worth of effort and planning—my wife's parents sold a vacation home and gave each of their children about $12,000 to spend as they wished. Sue immediately said, "Let's build an orphanage."

To which I replied, "What, are you crazy? We are on the brink of poverty ourselves!" This wasn't a completely accurate assessment of the situation, but the shock of losing so much money and continuing to lose for so long took its toll on my perception of my reality at the time.

Considering giving away the gift money was a very serious conflict between the facts: the fact that we were so broke, and our why, which was our reason for wealth in the first place. Somebody once said, "Adversity introduces a man to himself." I certainly just got introduced to myself, and it wasn't pretty.

By then we had been married for more than thirty years. Fairly early on we both learned that one of us usually had the right answer, an empowered, intelligent perspective. And if we paid close attention, we could both learn to recognize which one of us was thinking at a higher level. After our first and somewhat painful year of marriage, I discovered that it was less humiliating to intelligently acknowledge when she was right, rather than to have to apologize later for being such a jerk. I learned near the end of that first year that a more intelligent perspective was to be thankful that, at least half of the time, the Lord revealed the answer through my amazing wife. This was certainly one of those times. So I said, "Hon, I am seriously not seeing it… not even a little; but if you really feel in your heart that this is how we are to honor the Lord, I can agree, only because I trust you."

In our marriage, coming into agreement means that there will never be a time when either of us will say, "I knew we should never have done that…. I should have never let you talk me into it…. What was I thinking?" Rather, to agree means that we both commit to a decision and we stand together for the best outcome, and if it goes badly, it goes badly for both of us.

The organization Sue wished to send the money to had been successfully building orphanages in developing nations, and we had a deep personal relationship with the founders. The success of the organization had exploded exponentially to a degree that defies all reasonable expectation. As of today, AngelHouse.me has opened 151 homes, having rescued more than 4,000 children.

Many of us in this very blessed country are unaware that there are more people sold into slavery today than have been at any time in history. It's difficult to imagine places where children can be bought for as little as $20. Most of the little girls are sold into prostitution, and the boys will often not live to see their 20th birthday, being beaten as manual laborers. Those who escape slavery end up eating garbage found in the dumps and sleeping in the streets, which isn't much better. Because of cultural addictions and oppressive bondage, many of these children witnessed their drunken father murder their mother.

Quite surprisingly, at that time, $12,000 could build the nicest masonry home in the neighborhood, furnish it, and provide new clothing for 12 precious children, who had been living on the dirt streets or at the city garbage dump. Because of the passion and enthusiasm of the house parents, the home we financed opened with 18 children, and all were experiencing the gift of a lifetime! Another few thousand dollars could drill a well, providing safe, fresh water at the home, which typically then served everyone within walking distance, making the new home the center of life for the community.

On the day the home is opened, and the children run into their rooms for the first time, for most of them it is also the first time they have touched bedding. This is the first night they will have laid their heads on a pillow! It's hard for us to imagine, but since the children have never been loved or celebrated, almost all of them have no idea when they were born. On the day of the grand opening, a birthday party is celebrated for all of them, with cake, balloons, and presents, unlike anything they have ever experienced. It's all about them!

I wish you could have seen their faces! It was as though they had found themselves in heaven! And in spite of all the trauma that they lived through, their hearts were so pure and receptive to being loved.

Each home is established with the love of a married couple, who immediately become mom and dad to the whole family. Sue and I have had the pleasure of visiting them a few times. They send us their report cards and updates on their dreams and aspirations for life. It is as though the magnitude of their rescue elevated their value for life. They display a sense of destiny and purpose not often seen in those of us who never knew hopeless poverty. It is our expectation, and theirs, that these precious children will grow up to be doctors, lawyers, developers, investors, business people, entrepreneurs, and leaders in their nations. They certainly display the focus, drive, capacity, and commitment!

As a real estate investor myself, I think all of us are looking for the maximum impact at the lowest possible cost. Some things just naturally expand exponentially. While I do not claim to understand the psychology of going from great suffering to being loved, cared, and provided for, it has been an eye-opener to see how these children typically awaken to the reality of the gift that their lives can be to the world. They excel in school, become extraordinary citizens, and ascend to places of influence. They do not seem to be distracted with the accumulation of comforts but seem driven to fully capitalize the gift they have been given by becoming all they can, to be a gift to others.

One of my mentors, Russell Gray, says, "Do the math, and the math will tell you what to do." That's great advice for any investment! Seeing an opportunity to not only save a child from a torturous existence but also to launch them into a life of being a rich contributor to their nation and the world for just a couple thousand dollars felt like I had discovered the deal of a lifetime! I had never imagined that so great an impact could be accomplished with so little. I felt like I had struck gold!

In my world of real estate investing, the ultimate goal of each investment is the place in the timeline when our investors are enjoying infinite returns. What if the whole of life could be infinitely more impactful than expected? What if our investments themselves could make their own investments?

They say that "you can't take it with you," but what if you could? What if you could live your life in such a way that your greatest impact is after your time here is through and in a way that exponentially increases, like every good investment is expected to, into the generations to come. What if the purpose, passion, and profits that we have stewarded could be downloaded into the lives of our children and to those whom we mentor and impact?

What if? It's an interesting question, isn't it?

TWEETABLE
You can take it with you! Your impact can outlive your time on Earth!

Jerry Horst is a professional real estate investor, syndicator, philanthropist, and CEO of Vanguard Development Group, providing investment class real estate assets. See his son-in-law, Michael Manthei's chapter to understand infinite investment returns.

Jerry and his wife Sue have seven children, four grandchildren, and have traveled the world speaking on business, success, marriage and family. They are passionate about helping others find their passion and financial freedom.

Contact Jerry@vanguardDG.com.

CHAPTER 8

Ordinary Things Done Extraordinarily Well
My First Job

by Richard Rajarathinam

The year was 1991. I had recently moved from India to the United States to pursue my doctorate in theology. I first touched down on American soil in Washington, DC, and after some shuffling between Maryland and Mississippi, I ended up in Adelphi, Maryland. Hope was a flickering flame; everything I previously thought to be my future was shattered and the road ahead was dark. I was abandoned by the one person who was supposed to always be there for me. It felt like a betrayal—brutally painful and cruel. It was clear that this person whom I had counted on didn't understand how I felt nor did they understand the situation I was in at that time in my life. I had to deal with cold Maryland winter and the cold-heartedness of someone who I thought was supposed to be near and dear to me. They incriminated me because I had a girlfriend back in India that they didn't approve of. Furthermore, while continuing my post-graduate studies was the sole purpose of my migration to the USA, even that began to seem like an unobtainable fantasy.

It was time for me to face my bleak reality, so I hit the road. I needed to survive somehow. Walking down University Boulevard, I came across the Adelphi Shell gas station. I had no experience nor the slightest idea of how to fill out an application form for employment at the time, but I walked in blindly. I met the station manager, David, a very charming, blonde-haired, blue-eyed man with a dependency on cigarettes and a dictionary of curse words, both of which could be found in his mouth at all times. He helped me fill out the application. In the qualification section, I simply wrote these words: "Willing to do whatever." Those words were the seeds of what became a mantra for me: to do ordinary things extraordinarily well. That phrase coupled with the similarity between my and the owner's last name landed me a job. Although it only paid three dollars per hour, this job was my livelihood and my only means by which to survive.

On my first day of work, I was put behind the Gilbarco cash register to run the shift. Though it sounds simple, it was a monumental job for me at the time. I didn't even know the difference between a nickel and a dime. David's cursing and smoking over my shoulder didn't help either. I, coming from a conservative Indian pastor's family, had never experienced smoking in such proximity before. It made it very hard to breathe, but over the next few days, I learned that, despite our behavioral differences, he was a kind man. Under his management, I gave it my all working at that gas station. My desire to learn and my hard work was well appreciated too. Although I had a particular job title, I did whatever needed to be done around the station and gave it my best effort. I read in the Bible that whatever my hand finds to do, I was to do to the best of my ability. Even from a young age, I cultivated the desire to do more than was required of me and to do it well. I adhered to these qualities, and in turn, they would eventually lead me to what most people call success.

Within a few weeks, I was entrusted with the keys to the station to open the door in the morning and to close at night. I was punctual and demonstrated trustworthiness. There was not an elderly person who came to pump gas who left without me assisting them, checking their oil level and tire pressure, and cleaning their windshield. These little extra steps brought in a good amount of tips for me to buy myself vegetable fried rice from a nearby Chinese restaurant once in a while. No one had to tell me what to do during the day because I found something to do at all times, and I aimed to do it well. You couldn't find a single cigarette butt in the entire lot nor any weeds in the flower beds. I had a notorious habit of keeping all the curbs perfectly white and free from tire marks. I was out there almost every day touching up those scuffs with new paint. It wasn't just to impress people; these habits brought me real happiness as well. My reality at the time was bleak. I was sleeping in the mechanic bay of the gas station on a cardboard sheet from night to night because I had nowhere to go. However, I took pride in wearing the Shell uniform—grey pants and a tucked in white shirt with a yellow and red logo on it. Although it wasn't necessarily an honorable job, I embraced the opportunity that was presented to me and embraced the work I was doing. The red tie was not mandatory, but I made sure I wore it every day. This earned me a 100% rating from the mystery shoppers' evaluations that Shell sent. The store also consistently earned 100% for its appearance and customer service—scores like these were unheard of. Many of the customers started to write about the service that they received from me to the owner of the Shell station. The owner was a good man who we simply called "KK." He was an immigrant from Sri Lanka who came to the US sometime before me but understood what I was going through. He had visited me at the station a few times and was always brief but appreciative of my work. He had a lot of confidence in me. I later came to find that he owned four more gas stations.

KK had a habit of handwriting notes of appreciation on my paychecks. Those comments meant a lot to me, and I looked for them with great anticipation, sometimes even more than the amount on my paycheck. I was timid at the time and unable to show my genuine appreciation in return, but he knew I was happy to read those compliments. Today, I personally sign the checks for 150 employees of my own, and I never fail to write a comment of appreciation for a job well done. Simple things like this are very easy to do; however, they are just as easy to not do. It's in doing the little things like this that you can separate yourself from the ordinary and align yourself with the extraordinary. Eventually, I was appointed as manager to oversee three gas stations. This helped me to enroll in my doctoral study at the Howard School of Divinity. My flickering flame of hope revived. Yet, in spite of having to juggle classes and multiple shifts of work, I never missed a day nor did I ever complain.

Of the many memories I have of this period of my life, I recall one in particular that tested my integrity as a trustworthy and faithful employee and person. It was on a regular Monday morning. I always collected the money from the safe to deposit it in the bank at this time. However, on this occasion I was stunned to see there was no money in the safe. Normally, all the money accumulated over the weekend should have been there. It turns out that over the weekend at this gas station, the cashiers had plotted to get me in trouble by NOT dropping the cash that came in into the safe. The cashiers knew that other than the accountant, Nancy, only I had the combination for the safe. There would usually be around $10,000 in the safe after a weekend, so losing this lump of cash was far from a small issue. Police were called immediately, fingerprints were taken, and everyone was notified. Since I had just touched the safe to open it that morning, my fingerprints were still fresh and prominent on the safe. So, all evidence and speculation was pointed towards me. Even as I write this, I remember the situation very clearly—there was no way out. Circumstances surrounding the issues were enough evidence for me to be accused. I was a poor immigrant student in desperate need of money. It was then KK's turn to come make the final decision on whether or not they would turn me over to the authorities. It was then that KK said these words that I will never forget: "Even if $10,000 were sticking out of Richard's pocket right now, I would not believe that he stole the money." Tears of joy and relief poured out of my helpless eyes as I felt the rush of relief overcome me and I thanked God.

I began to move forward in life little by little. I was soon appointed to manager of the gas stations that KK owned. I continued to maintain my work ethic and was later honored as Shell corporation mid-Atlantic region employee of the month. After some time, KK had the idea to form a company called The Missing Piece in which he involved me heavily. The goal of this company was to promote motivational events and speakers such as Jim Rohn whom I drew a lot of inspiration from. It was through this job that I had the opportunity to meet Kyle Wilson. I was responsible for driving him to various appointments, and in that time, I shared some of my life stories with him. It was then, in 1993, that Kyle told me, "Richard, you must one day write a book." Here I am now writing this short story. It is a joy to partner with Kyle Wilson and write this chapter of *Purpose, Passion & Profit*.

God has been good to me, and I thank Him for this and all other blessings. I was able to graduate and receive my doctorate in ministry. I was able to unite with my then girlfriend, marry her, and have three wonderful children together. We have been happily married for 23 years. Today, I travel around the world, reach out to students in various countries, run my own business with 150 employees, and live a blessed life with my family. While I don't sleep on cardboard and fill gas anymore, those morals and values that I held dear back then are the same ones that push me every day. There is no "missing piece" to life's puzzle. What got me to where I am in life is simply doing the ordinary things that are easy to do extraordinarily well. Anyone can be ordinary, but to climb up the ladder to a successful life, one must take the extra steps to do those ordinary things extraordinarily well. This means picking up trash when you're on duty though it's not your job, being consistently punctual, showing genuine kindness to all people in everyday life and being truthfully reliable while demonstrating quality workmanship consistently. The good news about this is that anyone can do it. You don't need to have a degree to learn these basic virtues. There is nothing that makes me any more special than anyone else or more qualified for the kind of work I did than any other person. It's all about seeing your situation in a positive light, having faith in a brighter future, and doing every little thing in the here and now to your best.

TWEETABLE

There is no "missing piece" to life's puzzle. It is simply doing ordinary things extraordinarily well.

Dr. Richard Rajarathinam is the founder and CEO of Office Care Inc., a top 10 commercial cleaning company in the Washington, DC Metropolitan area. Although a businessman by trade, Richard's true passion is outreach. He travels around the world preaching and sharing his life stories to touch the lives of others and inspire youth. He considers this his ultimate profit. Contact him at richardraj@aol.com.

CHAPTER 9

How a Surgeon for Star Athletes Also Became a Multimillionaire Entrepreneur and Teacher

by Tom Burns, MD

"Can I really do that?!"

"This is just what I was looking for!"

These were comments from experienced, respected physicians who were acting like school kids at a birthday party.

I had just finished a presentation to a large group of physicians on money and the advantages of real estate. For many in the room this was new information, and they were clamoring to get more. They were excited, energized, and ready to take charge of their financial future. This highly intelligent group of professionals could not stop asking questions and would not let me leave the room. My teacher friends and I say that moments like these are when you realize you can make a difference!

I am an entrepreneur, a real estate professional, and an orthopedic surgeon. The last thing I expected was to become a teacher. Somewhere along the way I met some successful people, read some good books and discovered that making other people's lives easier was rewarding for everybody!

When I was young, all I thought about was sports. I eventually chose tennis, and since I had earned some statewide recognition, I thought I would one day be playing in the finals at Wimbledon. That didn't work out, so I decided the next best thing was to become an orthopedic surgeon and specialize in sports medicine. Sports medicine would keep me close to the action I loved and would still allow me to hang out with athletes I admired.

My career as a doctor was, and still is, fun and exciting. I have treated athletes from all over the world, many of whom have recognizable names. One of my most memorable moments was playing tennis with Martina Navratilova to get her back in shape after we operated on her knees! I have been, and continue to be, a physician for the United States Ski Team. That has allowed me to travel to faraway places and hang out with the best skiers in the world. My first ski team and Olympic experience was as the primary physician at the Olympic Training Center in Lake Placid. I was young and in shape, so I was invited to train with the aerialists. I was naturally adventurous, and I could not pass up the opportunity. I completed enough training jumps to qualify for competition but was never foolish enough to do it for real!

In the midst of all this fun, there was something missing. I noticed a consistent pattern in the way most doctors viewed their careers. Although they had impressive incomes, they were often complaining about time, money, and loss of control. As I considered the future, it was my impression that, while medicine was a noble calling, it was also potentially a declining industry and not a path to the financial freedom I craved. I began thinking that it might be smart to have a second stream of income that wasn't correlated to the medical industry. I did not want to feel trapped and unhappy as I got older, so I immediately started to research alternative sources of income.

After some early experimentation, it became clear that real estate was the perfect choice for my second stream of income. Real estate provided passive income, tax advantages, and a hedge against inflation. It could also be done part-time, and with or without partners. This fit the life of a full-time surgeon. However, I was never afraid to try other things. I was in multilevel marketing. I invested in medical and non-medical businesses. I tried the stock market. I owned a restaurant. I even spent time as a salesman for a magnetic lighter company.

Many of these efforts failed economically, but the experiences were not failures. In each venture, I learned a lesson that helped me move forward. In multilevel marketing, I learned sales, personal development, and overcoming fear of failure. The businesses that I invested in taught me the importance of management. The stock market taught me that it is best to have control over your investments. The lighter company taught me about sales and distribution. The restaurant business taught me about marketing and margins.

There were some trying times. My portfolio got killed in the dotcom crash in 2001 because I was following the advice of my financial planner. I had a lot of my money and my children's college funds tied up in the stock market. During that time, a famous mutual fund manager told me, "It would be impossible for the stock market to drop much lower!" Within 12 months, my stock holdings had dropped by 50%. That shaped my opinions about mutual fund managers and the stock market.

I also had some bad partners. One stole money and went to jail. Others were "ethically-challenged" or habitual liars. I learned that not everybody out there has your best interest at heart. Today, my two primary business partners are close friends whom I can trust with my life and my money. A good partner is worth his or her weight in gold!

By the time 2008 rolled around, I had learned a few lessons. I was still in the stock market, but I was more alert. I became uncomfortable with the subprime loan situation, and I exited the market shortly before it crashed. While gloating about saving my capital, I forgot to notice that I had multiple loans out to individuals and institutions for which I had personal guarantees. Access to capital dried up and those loans became due. I was terrified and embarrassed. For the first time in my life, I owed money and did not have the means to pay it back. Most of my cash flow had dried up, except for some well-positioned real estate. I had given my word that the money would be safe. Over the next two years, I took out several lines of credit, sold our family lake house, and used all my personal cash to make sure that all my investors were paid in full.

I could have worked on getting some of those loans eliminated, but my reputation was more important to me than the money. It took years to pay off those lines of credit. That was painful financially, emotionally, and personally as a husband and father. Our family's lifestyle became more limited, and I no longer had cash to take advantage of a real estate market in which everything was on sale. However, it was the right thing to do, and I maintained healthy, strong relationships with my friends and several banks. A few years later, those relationships would become profitable for me.

The lessons I learned from past mistakes and miscues allowed me to be successful enough in the real estate business to replace my physician income. Although I could have retired from medicine, I continue to practice to this day. I practice because I love what I do. I am blessed with the ability to meet dozens of people every day, form a relationship, and ease their pain. In parallel, as co-founder and principal of my private equity company, I meet new and exciting people every day in the form of partners, real estate professionals, and investors. Depending on the situation, I can ease their financial pain! I have had enough experience and made enough mistakes that it is now my mission to pass this knowledge on to other people, so they can avoid those pitfalls and create financial freedom faster than I did. I know it can be done!

I've had people label me as lucky. I do feel like a lucky guy, but my wife and my best friend say, "He makes his own luck." As Louis Pasteur stated, "Fortune favors the prepared mind." I don't know if my fortune has come so much from preparation as it has a little attention deficit without proper medication! Although it sounds like I bounced around without a plan, each project was always approached with the pursuit of excellence, faith in a higher power, and the notion that I would give my best effort. I knew that if I gave it 100% and learned along the way, it would be a successful journey. I've tried many different things that have led me down paths that I never expected to travel. Some have been dead ends, and others have led me to enrichment and fulfillment.

Some paths have connected me with friends that have been enormously successful. I'm privileged to meet twice a year with Robert Kiyosaki, author of *Rich Dad Poor Dad*, and his advisors. Robert and his advisors are real teachers. They are mission-driven, and they inspire me to be better. I'm friends with Gary Keller who has built the largest real estate brokerage company in the world and authored the enormously popular book *The One Thing*. Gary is a forward thinker, an innovator, and in my mind, somewhat of a philosopher. When we meet, we talk about family, guitars, and philosophy.

I develop as a person every time I have contact with quality people like this. I have been fortunate to associate with these great thinkers, entrepreneurs, and teachers. They are all givers, which is why they are successful. We are always taught that the more you give, the more you receive. We all need to make a living, but there is no disputing the material and relational success of serving and elevating others. When I speak to groups about real estate or personal development, I seem to get as much out of preparing for the talk and giving the speech as my audience does. If I'm giving valuable content to my audience and I'm improving myself as a result, what more could I ask for?

So, my story is not one of the doctor who turned into a real estate professional. I think it's the story of a physician turned entrepreneur who is becoming a teacher. I have reached many of my financial and personal development goals. Now the fun part is expanding my mind to continually set these goals higher. There is so much to learn and so much to share that I see no reason to stop. I thought that when I got the money I would be done, but I am pulled to do more. Today, my real estate company acquires or develops $100 million of prime property per year. We have a great team that allows me to pursue all my goals. I love the action, but there is more to give. If I want to elevate others, I must keep learning, teaching, and growing.

What can you do? My suggestion is to seek teachers, never stop learning, and pass it on. You will enrich yourself and those around you. You can make a difference!

TWEETABLE

I have had enough experience and made enough mistakes that it is now my mission to pass this knowledge on to other people so they can avoid those pitfalls and create financial freedom faster than I did.

Tom Burns, MD is an orthopedic surgeon who created his financial freedom through a multimillion-dollar real estate portfolio. He is a principal and co-founder of a successful real estate private equity firm. His mission is to teach others how to find their path to success using some of the same lessons he learned on his journey. He frequently speaks to physician and professional groups about life, money, and real estate. To book him for a speaking engagement or podcast, email info@presarioventures.com or visit www.presarioventures.com.

CHAPTER 10

Leaning Too Far Out The Window

by Chad Hughes

All is well. It was the summer of 2014, and I was sitting on the patio with my dad talking about the exciting entrepreneurial things that were happening for me. We had been expanding my land and environmental consulting business across Canada, I was involved in launching a couple of startups, and I was dabbling with some small-scale real estate. This was my passion. The growth, variety, experiences, learning, and the people I was hanging with had me feeling on top of the world.

My dad was cautioning me about the risk involved in everything I was doing and how passion can be deceiving. You see, my dad was once a passionate entrepreneur who had built an empire and later dismantled it. As a kid, I had experienced both the ups and the downs, the downs being devastating to all of us. My dad was concerned that I was on a similar path, a path that would eventually take my energy and passion away if I wasn't careful.

I was so high about my progress that I insisted I had it covered when, little did I know, I was 12 months away from almost losing it all.

My Entrepreneurial Journey

I started a career in land acquisition at 20 years old. I began acquiring interests in land for the oil and gas industry. I was in over my head, but I had been raised on a farm by a man who, more than anything, had taught me how to work really hard and persevere. Six years later I was presented with the opportunity to join a newly started land company with an option to buy in, and six months later I was invested. I was 26 years old and about to start my adult entrepreneurial journey.

The road ahead would have more ups than downs and would increase my entrepreneurial confidence. I started to dabble within my current business and outside of it with real estate. In my spare time, I was acquiring property, flipping homes, and developing on a small scale. Ignorant to the risks, I was winning. It was fuel.

The ideas came from everywhere, and I began reaching further, taking more risks. Someone planted the seed about taking the executive MBA, so I did. That experience alone seemed to triple my capacity, and things took off. I would see a cool product and buy the rights. I would see a cool franchise concept and buy an area. If I got the slightest whiff of an opportunity, I was all in. My vision became more than building the best land and environmental business in Canada and evolved into mastering multiple businesses.

At a certain point, I heard about the Entrepreneur Organization (EO) and became a member. There I would gain insight into my innate abilities and meet some remarkable people, which motivated me further. I met Peter Thomas, a well-known entrepreneur who founded Century 21 Canada and built the Four Seasons in Scottsdale, Arizona among a long list of other amazing accomplishments. Peter became a mentor and friend whose wisdom and influence only added to my confidence.

Through Peter, I met other successful entrepreneurs, like Dave LaRue who would become my coach. I was hanging with guys in the big leagues with high net worth and feeling like I was on the same playing field. I wasn't, but I was filled with passion and an inflated ego to support my ambitions.

A Punch in the Nose

The wheels of growth would begin to wobble when I received news that one of our largest national land acquisition projects was being put on hold. This was the start of what would turn into the most challenging times for me as an entrepreneur and personally. Unaware, I was leaning too far out the window.

Then, on November 27, 2014 the Organization of Petroleum Exporting Countries decided not to cut oil production levels and would attempt to squeeze out other world producers. This sent the price of oil into a tailspin. The political environment was changing in Canada as well. Both were very bad for business, but I wasn't ready to accept fact.

The following 12 months were difficult, but the land business was doing okay. Then on month 14, the other shoe dropped. What seemed like overnight, we started hitting lows we had never seen before. Clients were cutting budgets to zero and at the same time demanding 30% reductions to the fees we charged. When reality hit me in the face, I was in full reactive mode, chasing a declining business for the next 12 months.

The impact was devastating. We said goodbye to a lot of our staff. There were many sleepless nights spent worrying about the personal situations and families of the people relying on the business for their livelihoods. No visibility for what was around the corner led to other conflicts. Partner relationships were strained, people were afraid, morale was in decline, and my leadership was waning.

I began to realize what my dad was warning me about as the pressure of being stretched mounted. My land and environmental business needed 150% of my focus, while I had other businesses to navigate. A financial partner pulled out of one of them because of the business environment. Faced with the worst recession on record, I was left to sort things out on my own. To keep it all afloat, I began divesting of real estate assets to the point where there wasn't much left. I was running on fumes, in massive debt, in the middle of a terrible tax audit, and worst of all, I was lacking clarity and energy.

The Toll

The events took a toll on me. I am an optimist and see opportunity everywhere I look, generally believing I can accomplish anything; I stopped seeing and believing. When I am in, I am all in; I wanted out. I am a growth guy always moving forward, and although usually I help others see the exciting future I see, I was stalled and wasn't inspiring anyone. When I get my hands into an idea, I easily connect the dots to make the idea a reality; I couldn't connect. My energy levels are naturally high and my mood bright; I was dragging my ass.

I was losing my vision, questioning my abilities, and feeling like a fraud, as if I had been fooling myself up until this point. My daily habits became less of a priority. I wasn't meditating consistently or thinking the best thoughts, and I was drinking more. I felt very alone and struggled to connect with myself.

Eventually, I stopped talking about our company vision and my own. The amount of focus required was intense, yet my strength and energy was out the window. Looking back, it was a very dark time.

Recovering

I did maintain a few good habits. I consistently worked with my coach, Dave LaRue, and started having breakthroughs. One of these breakthroughs helped me avoid complete financial ruin. I began to understand how my dad's experiences impacted my own thinking. I came to the realization that I was in this situation because I had allowed myself to be. I came to realize how good I am at ignoring reality when it doesn't match how I see life.

I realized that I wasn't paying enough attention to my vision gap. The gap is the territory between your current place and the one you see in the future. That gap needs to be addressed for a vision to become real. I realized I was avoiding difficult decisions, and I worried too much about what others thought of me. I started being honest with myself and looking closely at how I was contributing to the situation.

I stayed close with God through the journey. There were many prayers answered, albeit not always the way I wanted. In many respects, I believe I was supposed to go through this in preparation for the bigger part of God's plan for me.

These realizations and habits eventually saved me. As my habits grew stronger, my discipline grew, my clarity improved, and my thinking improved. I started taking massive action on things, and in time our business improved. The experience changed me, strengthened me, and has prepared me for the next level.

Now, in 2018, we are back in a growth mode. I have a clear vision and a stronger team around me to achieve it. I am connecting the dots and taking action. I am playing in my genius again and enjoying being an entrepreneur.

Lessons Learned for the Next Chapter

I have come to appreciate that the hardest times have been my times of greatest growth. Too much was accomplished to mention it all and so much was learned. I will share what stands out.

Less Is More

The joy of pursuing opportunity comes from seeing progress and growth resulting from your efforts. When you are spread thin, you don't have an opportunity to give enough to the process of moving your ideas forward. The lack of focus ends up robbing you of some of the joy involved in advancing a new opportunity.

When you're open, there will be an abundance of opportunity, and it's okay to let some pass by. It's better to ensure you are squeezing everything possible out of the things you're involved in and to ensure you have the capacity to do so. As a result of these events, I have become aware of the effort and energy required to make an idea reality, and I am more aware of my own limitations.

Ego

It turns out I have an ego, and I didn't realize how dangerous this could be until I reflected on its role. Ego will prevent you from seeing the truth about yourself, and in some cases your situation. My ego was telling me I was different and was fueling an over-confidence that was unfounded, and it cost me.

Today I pray on this daily and watch for places where ego shows up. It's usually in my head, but if it's in my head it's affecting my thinking, and my thinking influences my actions. It's simply an awareness thing for me now, and it's making a positive difference.

Belief Alone Is Not Enough
I was relying on belief more than actions, and belief alone doesn't produce results. I wasn't paying enough attention to the vision gap and the difficult decisions that would need to be made to close that gap. My vision wasn't clear enough in every aspect of my life, which meant that some important pieces weren't moving forward or getting appropriate attention.

Today, I have described my vision across every aspect of my life, spiritual, vocational, relationship, financial, and social. I start each day with a question, and that question is, *What am I going to do today to close the gap?* I keep a clear view of the future and turn my focus to the present and moving the needle. Daily progress is my objective.

Refusing Reality
I learned that I have the ability to brush off reality. I cringe at the slightest sign of negativity and mistake real talk for negativity. When you don't face reality, you don't make the right decisions, and some decisions are crucial to your success and survival.

Today I ask more questions and I listen. When life doesn't match the way I think it should, I get clear on why and turn my energy to finding a way to get things back on track, quickly.

Habits
Dave LaRue says sometimes your habits work so well you forget why you have them. I should have been doubling down on my best habits, and I wasn't. I don't know the reason, but perhaps the pressure I was under started a slow slide away from what helped me become successful in the first place, and it was slow enough that I couldn't see it.

Today my habits are followed consistently, and I am aware of how easily they can slip. Slip an inch and you will soon slip a mile. I incorporate the habits I want into my quarterly plan and articulate what these success habits are at the start of each week. It helps me keep them front of mind. If you want your life to change, stop what you're doing, and do something different. Your life won't change if you don't.

Don't Let Others Decide Who You Are
It turns out I do care what other people think of me. I like to be liked, I care how others perceive me, and at times I am easily influenced. This is a problem when you're faced with making difficult or unpopular decisions. I was losing confidence when others were not pleased with me, which made it hard to take the steps that were crucial to my survival.

I now accept that some decisions will be painful to make, and I realize that I will be judged more on the how than the what. I realize that people will also judge you for the decisions you don't make. It's a work in progress for me.

Aha Moments

I received guidance from some amazing people, and their coaching has been a major factor in my survival and adaptation. I have come away with clarity on how much I love learning and growing, how much I love teaching and influencing, and how much I love sharing and helping others with their journey. I have clarity on how these things I love create value for my clients, in my business, and to the people surrounding me.

The future I see is one in which I continue to create environments where others will have an opportunity to connect with their own entrepreneurial gifts. I see an environment where I am mindfully coaching the people around me and perhaps other entrepreneurs who are searching for their own answers. I see a future where I am helping others connect with their genius and leveraging my own genius to take all aspects of my life to the next level. I see myself able, able to make a difference to others. I see myself ready, ready to take things to the next level. I see myself building, building great businesses and great people and loving every minute of every day.

TWEETABLE

Appreciating the value of your greatest challenges is a choice that is crucial in going to the next level. It can lead you to the truth about who you are and what you love, and that truth will set you free.

Chad Hughes pours his entrepreneurial passion into LandSolutions as President and CEO. LandSolutions provide land acquisition, stakeholder engagement, environmental, and asset management services to the energy, telecommunication, infrastructure, and real estate industries across North America. Chad's other entrepreneurial endeavours include real estate, a health supplement product line called Dynamis, and a canine hospitality franchise called Dogtopia.

Chad sees how entrepreneurial environments expedite a person's growth and is passionate about creating them and helping people find their entrepreneurial genius through writing, coaching, or simple experience sharing. Reach out on LinkedIn https://www.linkedin.com/in/chadhughesland/ or by email at chad@hc-group.ca.

CHAPTER 11
Millionaire by 24
Discovering the Science Behind Living with Clarity, Empathy, and Owning It

by Erika Feinberg

How does a child of a math whiz, stockbroker father and an opera singer, radio personality, and angel of a mother turn out? My dad was one of the original employees of Merrill Lynch and did quite well there his entire adult life in his own maverick way. My dad and mom involved me in their days. My mom always encouraged me to be my wonderful self. Her radio show pulled me into meeting people like Sammy Davis Jr., Jack Benny, and many more. My mom never made a big deal of the show business piece. She kept us away from watching too much TV and pop culture by involving us with life: sailing, horseback riding, the arts. She always practiced and preached philanthropy and saw the concept of entertainment as being the art of touching people and positively influencing lives.

My three older brothers and I were raised by the same people in the same place but each of us grasped much different memories of our lives, and we all turned out radically different! My oldest brother is very spiritual and a brilliant freehand artist. My second brother went into the medical field, built a solid family, passionately influenced improvements in his community in the Hamptons, and later committed suicide. My third big brother became a financial planner straight out of college and is an exceptionally solid, traditional, and generous human. Then there's me. As a child, Wall Street influenced my choices of breakfast cereal. I was a curly-haired, freckled-faced blonde forging through life with rose-colored glasses on. I lived each day with no fear, an abundant amount of energy, good luck, and smiles. I just always had a knack for soaking in information at the speed of light, connecting with people, treasuring every second, identifying market needs, crafting plans, and manifesting happiness and success for everyone involved. **Despite some major shit storms I've chosen to ignore**, everything I'm sharing with you represents my choice of what is deeply etched into my core.

I grew up to build three well-loved, multimillion-dollar market-leading businesses; the latest one generating over $90 million before I sold it in 2014. I also co-founded a venture philanthropy non-profit that has donated high tens of millions and endless amounts of operational expertise to non-profits around the world. My unique approach has been awarded and included in case studies by programs such as Kauffman Foundation's FastTrac, SCORE, AMEX, and UPS.

I identified a winning formula, and it's what I call a MastermindTNT. I've somehow been motivated by the right inner fire and with a highly productive mindset which, if you get close enough to, becomes contagious. Over the years, I've gotten it down to a science and noticed that solidifying stories and grasping certain concepts helps others drive huge wins. My rose-colored glasses approach somehow makes it seem fun and easy.

Despite their polar differences, I became half my mom and half my dad, and life became one big radio show for me. I'd question the Rabbi in our temple, my teachers, parents…. I always had to know why. I'd ask, "What does that mean to you?" or "How can that help?" or "Why is that bad?" to process information. I also had to learn how to make my own decisions because my mom and dad were polar opposites. So I learned how to visualize my end goal and how to craft proposals with mass appeal to win yeses from my family and other stakeholders. It didn't occur to me until I pursued my master's degree in human dynamics (2016) that this empathetic aspect of my personality and of my decision-making style (crawling into people's heads first) was likely born from our family dynamics and has played a big part in my personal and professional success ever since. I was a fancy-free, rambunctious opportunist through these years of my life, and **I was so blinded by a bigger purpose, I never noticed if I failed at anything**. I could have turned out any which way. I just chose to own the ground I stood on and was fueled by making a difference in other people's lives.

Four major events changed everything for me. I was the white blonde minority attending a diverse school with lots of drugs and misdirected kids. I loved to learn and loved to "explore" people, so I learned how to win everyone over, see the best in everyone, and earn straight A's while staying "cool." My parents moved me from this very rough public high school, Brien McMahon in Norwalk Connecticut, into St. Luke's Private School in New Canaan my senior year. St. Luke's brought me brilliant, accomplished mentors, discussion-based classrooms, and a passionate drive for achievement as the norm. **The norm at Saint Luke's was to utilize your body, communication skills, and data for impact, and to connect it to a purpose in the world. This really sums up what "MastermindTNT" is.** That school felt like home to me, but most everyone there was bonded together since seventh grade. They were so polished, so motivated, and so smart, from all walks of life! I don't think I cared that I was an outsider, and I wasn't afraid, but I do remember feeling "below" them in a very logical way. All I know is, I decided to LOVE it; I graduated at the top of my class, and it brought me to Boston University. I LOVED it! If I didn't have that experience, I can't even imagine what my life would look like today.

The second major growth blessing for me was meeting Larry Ellison, then Ted Turner, and simultaneously serving both Oracle Corporation and Turner Broadcasting during their biggest years of major transition…and helping them transform those businesses into massive market leaders. I was a new college grad in my 20s. I was earning a pittance plus performance bonuses while my friends were getting big salaries from big companies. While I felt a little uncomfortable and like an outlier, I wasn't afraid. I lived with clarity. I was intuitive and empathic, and a faith-filled Energizer Bunny. I opened these relationships with carefully crafted decisions and strategic win-win plans, just like I did as a kid. Oh, and it didn't occur to me that my prospects would be anything but thrilled that I was in their lives.

Then, Ray Lane came into my life. He became President and COO of Oracle and drove a massive strategic and cultural shapeshift of the company through the 90s. Do your research…he's one of the most spectacular leaders on this Earth in my eyes. After assigning me a very aggressive project involving $150 million in value, he would say, "I have all the confidence you will be able to deliver results by Thursday." To say the least, the first few moments were secretly terrifying. However, his style quickly directed me into a can-do mindset that always worked! My performance bonuses far surpassed anything my friends were making. **When I was barely through feeling like a misfit, I became a millionaire in my early 20s.**

During this decade plus, I was struck by the women like Dana Gould at Logix (my first real job in Waltham, MA) and the women Oracle had in power positions: Safra Catz, Polly Sumner, and others. **They all shared similar characteristics of intense clarity and drive that, unbeknownst to me at the time, seeped into my soul.** I didn't realize the impact these women had on me until I was invited onto a radio show in 2015 that is run by a "woman for woman" business leader. During the pre-interview, this radio host asked me if I thought Oracle was sexist. I answered "No!" and told her why. Well, that got me dis-invited for some mysterious reason, which got me quite angry, but not for reasons you might think! I was upset this radio host was in a power position to influence women, and she was perpetuating the wrong perspectives! **Really think about the meaning of "wrong perspective."** You might agree with me, or you might agree with her, but ask yourself, **which perspective serves your life and your goals better?**

That's how I define right and wrong. 100% of the perspectives that nourish my life and those around me are allowed. **I work hard to replace depleting perspectives with something more nourishing.**

These perspectives and accomplishments led me to be appointed to a new position at Arizona State University (ASU) called Entrepreneur in Residence (2015-16). Teaching leadership, innovation, and entrepreneurship ignited my passion for what I coined "interactive and purpose-based teaching." I leaped into ASU with a plan to put my model of success to the test with these students as I did with my employees, and it worked! I started by working on their life stories and helped light their lives on fire by helping them connect their knowledge and passions to the real world. I didn't understand why academia didn't see that data needed to be connected to purpose for it to be significant! ASU won "most innovative" award from US News and World Report the year I was there. Student venture teams were winning venture funding. I also helped a couple of students to choose not to drop out and in two extreme cases not to commit suicide by helping them connect the best iteration of their life story and their passions to a real purpose. So, it was a dream blessing that brought me closer to the MastermindTNT mindset. Why was I so good and happy?

The title of this book starting with purpose speaks to me. Purpose comes first, and our choice of stories or core beliefs, fuels our passion to our goals.

What do I mean by core beliefs? The third major experience in my life that knocked everything up a level happened during a Club Med ski vacation when I was in my mid-20s. I was an experienced skier and ski racer, skiing double black diamond runs and ungroomed bowls. But I grew up out east, skiing aggressively with consistent surprise ice patches, and I was taught to lean forward and use my edges. I moved out west, and my skiing abilities unraveled. I just couldn't lean back and relax. It sounds simple, right? I was getting stuck in the snow, I was falling, and I just couldn't lean back and adjust! So many years of aggressive eastern skiing and experiences of surviving ice patches conditioned me deeply. **I was stuck in my head.**

For two weeks we were skiing with some of the best skiers in the world. I was starting to get the hang of it, but with fear and resistance running through my head. I didn't realize I was becoming the talk of the French and Swiss instructors. They saw I had skills and strength. They just couldn't penetrate my head and affect my beliefs. One day, my instructor Jean Pierre said to me with a strong French accent, "It's time you pretend you are a great, confident, and beautiful skier like me. Let's do this today. Let's do this right now." We had just gotten new snow, so leaning back would mean my shoulders would be touching the snow on these double black diamond trails! Well, I skied behind Jean Pierre (as my role model), and I tried it. **I didn't realize that following him and just smiling, relaxing, and pretending the right way could completely displace my fear and beliefs with something else. That iteration of pretending has been fueling my life ever since.**

"Pretending" in this context is as real as it gets. I became a confident, beautiful skier, enjoying the bumps and flying through the air, even with my shoulders touching the snow. I also felt accountable to Jean Pierre and his peers, so I had to do it. It was just a matter of my thoughts getting in the way. This type of breakthrough is not easy though. These beliefs run deep! From this experience I learned how to be an even better mentor and teacher by inspiring, encouraging, and distracting my audience in just the right way and leveraging "the village" to get it done.

The fourth, but not last, major milestone event in my life was my brother's suicide. It was absolutely a "life's too short" lesson. He was living in the Hampton's with a beautiful, best friend wife and two amusing, talented, and passionate kids you'd love and crave. He was the brother who took me under his wing and taught me to stay alert, to be impatient, to stay healthy, to forge and win, and to impact every second and every person I touch. His death could have paralyzed me, but I chose to leverage it as my "differentiated fuel." I still miss him, and this tragedy became my "fabric." It became my responsibility to make productive sense of what happened. Everyone my brother's decision affected kept asking endless questions that he was not here to answer for us. We all could have easily driven ourselves crazy trying to find the answers! This circles back to my comment about **replacing depleting perspectives with something more nourishing.** I just got to a point in which I chose to leverage the pain to create a tremendous amount of happiness and success for everyone in my world. Life's a very unique blessing and a responsibility that I cherish. I realize that my skills and ambition are insignificant unless they're being used productively with the right people and to notable levels of potential.

I now measure my success by the impact I can have on those around me, my chosen "village." I've learned that my audience has to be ambitious professionals, lovable, intuitive, and empathic people, and life-long learners.

Of everything I could have chosen to tell you, including the major shit storms, these particular stories spilled out of me because they've supported my wins and can help you too. **Do you see how the stories you choose to internalize support who you are, how you think, how you impact others,**

and what your life looks like today? MastermindTNT represents the mindset and science behind performance, effective communications, and lofty goal achievement; I just happened to be good at implementing it and imparting the art of it. **If we want more from life, let's reflect on it and let's tell stories that fuel your life's vision.**

TWEETABLE

MastermindTNT starts in your mind and works its way out through your heart. Pretending you're amazing while you're accomplishing something amazing is as real as it gets. Changing your mind changes your life.

ERIKA FEINBERG: Has been CEO of three small businesses which she grew into multi-million, market-leading, and nationally loved brands. Her latest business generated over $90 million in revenue. She coaches—on-stage and on-site—in her fun, very interactive, content-rich style…and she helps corporate clients power through organizational change, new launches, and lofty goal achievement.

B.S. Communications and Business, Boston University

M.S. Human Dynamics, Western International University.

To book Erika to speak on your stage, to run a MastermindTNT workshop for your teams, or to put a total-solution in place for your enterprise:

Ask@ApexOutcomes.com

www.ApexOutcomes.com

CHAPTER 12

How I Went from Jumping out of Military Airplanes into Multimillion Dollar Investments!

by Elijah Vo

"Love your family, work super hard, live your passion."

– Gary Vaynerchuk

t's especially difficult to sum up someone's life with a quote, but I love this quote because it combines family, dedication, and ambition, three concepts that explain why I do what I do. Family. Hard work. Passion. BAM! Those three phrases illustrate a relational, focused, and motivated purpose. I've actually used these three concepts as my purpose in progressing from an Army grunt, sleeping in the mud to a successful, multifamily real estate investor. I've leveraged many other concepts to grow and improve, but the messages behind these words have been so vital they are the focus of my story.

Love your family. This concept is the key for me. Your success in this life depends on your ability to define and understand your "why." When you have massive, outlandish goals (which I often do), you have to develop a thorough understanding of what fuels your passions, so you don't quit when you're being put to the test. My family is my number one why. I have many whys, but family is the biggest.

When I first started investing in real estate, I did it for material reasons. I thought becoming "rich" would lead to happiness. I frankly misunderstood both wealth and happiness. I also really didn't understand how to anchor my goals around something meaningful, like family.

As I grew as an investor, however, I began to realize that accumulating money alone wouldn't motivate me when the going got tough. Money is a great primal motivator, but I found that the thought of simply having money for its own sake would not propel me forward when I was tired and frustrated and wanted to call it quits. So I had to ask myself, "Why do this?"

The answer was my family. My wife. My son. My daughter. All of them depended on me for love and support. I couldn't fail them. Money was not the goal, but it was the tool I needed to build my family an extraordinary life. So I changed my mindset. My desire for wealth quickly became a quest to create financial freedom so we could live life by our own design. The new "why" of family has made all the difference for me, which leads me to my next concept.

Work super hard. You need to be 1000% committed to the grind to achieve success. Work super hard every day without complaining, because it can always be worse. I can thank my military career for this mindset. Originally, I didn't aim to be an entrepreneur. In fact, right out of high school I joined the US Army. As if that wasn't enough, I somehow thought it would be a good idea to jump out of perfectly good airplanes, as a paratrooper. I made a career of sorts by sleeping in the mud and kicking in doors.

This life was so different, but yet involved a lot of hard work. I remember, 18 years ago, standing in the doorway of an Air Force C-130 cargo aircraft as we approached our drop zone in Anchorage, Alaska. The jumpmaster was standing next to me. The red light was still lit. The doors were wide open, and freezing air was rushing into the belly of the plane. We were each loaded up with 100lbs of equipment, preparing to jump into a field exercise in the middle of winter. I was the lucky first jumper. Hooah! The jumpmaster tightened his grip on my shoulder in anticipation; that meant we were close. I quickly looked around. Everyone was either wide-eyed or praying…I probably should have been too. I caught my Commander's glance, and he gave me a nonchalant smile. Just then, green light! The jumpmaster slapped my shoulder while yelling, "Go! Go! Go!"

I often laugh at those memories because they're drastically different from where I am now. Polar opposite. I wouldn't recommend that path to everyone, but it was great for me because I had tons of ambitious energy at 18 years old, but very little direction. The Army helped me focus a lot of the super hard work into something productive. It put me in situations that mentally and emotionally drained me, but I had to force myself to work beyond my limits—a characteristic that is critical in what I do now. I learned that you can be smart; you can have dreams; you can even have money, but if you don't work super hard, you won't get anywhere.

After my second tour, I left the Army to pursue college and corporate America. I thought I had found direction. I believed that going to college, getting good grades, and working for someone else was a sure path to success. I suppose I defined "success" as staying out of debt and saving 20 or 30 years so I could retire. A lot of people do, but something about that philosophy never sat right with me.

So I spent two years in college, and then I realized I actually missed serving in the military. I was no longer excited about jumping out of airplanes, but I did enjoy the hard work found in the military. I re-enlisted, this time in the Air Force as part of its IT sector. I needed a prominent career in a challenging, fast-paced industry to match my energy and curiosity, so technology seemed to be the logical choice. Little did I know, it was at this point that my mindset would undergo one of its most dramatic transformations that would ultimately guide my family and career to its current path of success!

Live your passion. I found my passion in the Air Force. I think this part of the quote is last because it's the concept that makes the whole philosophy work. If you're not passionate about what you do, it does not matter what moves you. It does not matter how hard you work. Something has to change. The first thing to change should be you.

I was extremely excited about my new IT job. We were saving money and I was working towards a "happy" life and (hopefully) a retirement. I made some new friends and felt like I had it figured out. However, every day at work, I would talk with one of those friends, a guy named Harold, about wealth, finance, and business. These talks helped change my perspective.

Harold didn't talk about money the same way everyone else in our unit did. He talked about long-term goals like investing, wealth building, business, economics, and education—subjects nearly revolutionary in a military culture. His insight and mindset were fascinating to me. We spent the next year talking almost every day. Slowly my mindset began to shift from a wage-earning mindset to one focused on breaking from that, setting higher goals, building wealth, and creating financial freedom. This is where I learned one of the most important lessons of success: before you change your life, you have to change your mindset.

Eventually, my wife and I started our first real estate investing company, EVO2 Enterprises LLC. We prioritized our education, expanded our network, and purchased two single-family rentals. We ultimately wrote a 25-page business proposal that outlined our five-year plan to leverage single-family flips and rentals to purchase small multifamily units. Within ten years, we planned to purchase large multifamily deals as large as 20-30 units!

We started socializing and networking with other like-minded people. Through those connections, we met our mentors and now good friends, Mark and Tamiel Kenney of Think Multifamily, an investing and educational group out of Dallas, TX.

We met Mark and Tamiel at one of their Meetups in Grapevine, TX (now, I co-host that Meetup with them). I remember telling him our 20-unit plan and him asking me, "Eli, why buy 20 units when you can buy 200?" Mark has probably asked hundreds of people that same question, but it definitely set the tone for that conversation and for how I invest in real estate today.

I rushed home and told my wife about this amazing couple. She was excited too! We went back to Mark and Tamiel, who have been so kind in helping us expand our focus and remain goal oriented. I learned early another key fact of success: to operate at the highest levels, you need mentors and a strong inner circle to push and support you. I was 1000% committed and tried to absorb as much as I could from them, all the while providing value wherever I could to them.

Coincidently, I deployed to the Middle East that year. Life was complicated but, I remembered to love my family, work hard, and stay passionate. I would wake up early or stay up late to complete both my military duties and investment goals. I was living my passion, and that made it easier. I learned such powerful, wealth-building techniques of commercial real estate, mostly one-on-one with Mark and Tamiel. I loved what I was doing and was willing to grind until I met my goals.

I returned home from the desert, joined Think Multifamily's Inner Circle/ Mastermind program, and partnered with an ambitious investor named Brent. The hunt for deals was on! Since then, Brent and I have scoured the markets, analyzed countless deals, and worked a lot of extra hours looking for "the deal." We've toured properties during our lunch and off times and even hopped on a couple of one-day flights to check out potential deals.

Our persistence, hard work, and sacrifice has paid off! As I'm writing this chapter, Mark, Brent, and I are closing on our first 100+ unit deal in Atlanta, GA! We have closed the contract, completed our due diligence, and are in the process of raising money. We expect to close sometime in the next couple of months.

During this journey, I have learned a ton of lessons. I learned the journey is just beginning. Here is my advice to you: your dreams begin with a **purpose**. It takes commitment, time, and lots of sacrifice to crush your goals, so you have to dig deep down every day and remember why you started. It's okay to start with a dream, but eventually you have to muster the courage to take massive action. Take action today and do not stop until your goal is accomplished. To take this leap, you need a **passion** so intense that nothing, minus God himself, can stop you! Work super hard and never let your doubts and failures thwart your progress. Your goals will take time and extreme focus to accomplish, so don't let impatience or lack of focus weaken your drive.

Lastly, think about your last five conversations. Ask yourself "Did those conversations get me closer to accomplishing my goals?" If the answer is no, then you need to surround yourself with people who support your goals and force you to level up. Provide them with as much value as you can. The renowned Jim Rohn has said, "Your net worth is equal to your network." These seven words are so profound because you will not obtain the desired **profits** without a professional network of like-minded, high achievers to help you chase that dream. Good luck, and I'll see you at the grind!

TWEETABLE

It takes commitment, time, and tons of sacrifice to crush your goals.... It's okay to start with a dream, but eventually you have to muster the courage to take massive action. Take action today and do not stop until your goal is accomplished.

Elijah Vo began in real estate by investing in single-family rentals with his wife, Ebannie. His passion to build their family's wealth catalyzed them into multifamily real estate where they are invested in over 900 units. Elijah is an IT Project Manager in the US Air Force, where he has proudly served for 15+ years. Elijah has a B.A. in Business Administration from Columbia College and is a member of the Fort Worth Chamber of Commerce. You can connect with him at evo2enterprises@gmail.com.

CHAPTER 13

Hitting the Leadership Wall, Releasing the False Expectations of Others

by Kevin Ozee

C ontrol what you can control. Have a good attitude. Give maximum effort. These are much easier preached than lived, at least in my case. It took me two major crises within a year to make me realize my true purpose, passion, and profit.

So, there I was at the pinnacle of my twenty-plus year public education career. The last sixteen I spent as an administrator and I had worked my tail off to move up and stay ahead. Due to my teams' and employees' successes over the years, national awards and recognition had been bestowed upon me. I had recently returned to my hometown to lead a department of almost 400 staff members and 15,000 student-athletes. The support from the community was immense, and I felt it every day.

However, something very ugly was brewing inside of me. As most men my age and older do, I tied my identity to my job. Growing up, I was a mediocre student and a mediocre athlete. Looking back, I was also a mediocre coach and a mediocre classroom teacher in my early career. However, due to my mentor and friend's untimely death, at the young age of 33, I was promoted to a role of leadership at a very successful athletic program with very successful coaches. The coaches I inherited, most with much more experience and skins on the wall than me, are now in many Hall of Fames and considered legends in their respective sports.

Looking back, my first few years in a leadership role were on the job training. Most of the learning came by expensive, negative experiences. I was a worse leader than I was a student, athlete, or classroom teacher. I knew that I had to work my tail off to improve every day and to prove myself. I had to prove myself to coaches under my watch who were skeptical of a young, know-nothing guy who was their new boss. I had to win their respect and approval. Work ethic, constantly seeking improvement, and success generated by successful people on my staff brought acclaim that I received way too much credit for as an individual. I was named the National Association for Sports and Physical Education's 2013 National High School Athletic Director of the Year, our teams won 21 state championships, and three straight Texas University Interscholastic League's Lone Star Cups. While athletic director at Duncanville ISD, *Sports Illustrated* named our program a national Top 25 high school program.

My innate desire to provide for my family a lifestyle I never knew growing up pushed me. My identity to try to be the best in my job was a daily burden. I didn't even realize the toll it was taking on my subconscious mind and my physical body. Over time, my true, introverted personality was crumbling inside my very public, extroverted work world. I was living one way at home and pretending to be the warrior-hunter-gatherer at work. During the day I was William Wallace in *Braveheart*, ready to take on the world, fighting the battles as the general leading the charge for the greater good. I was having to prove myself over and over again to my bosses, the community, and the people I served.

At home, I was the complete opposite. I had given up on exercise, trying to eat healthy, and staying in touch with the ones I love. I was a broken record to my boys and an absent husband to my wife. Honey, it wasn't that I was not listening to disrespect you. I just didn't care anymore. Warning to all: basing your identity on your career is a trainwreck waiting to happen.

If my story is cliché, I cannot apologize to you. Keep reading, as it may save your life, your marriage, and your relationships with those you love the most. I suppose my story is not uncommon to men my age, as I have seen men who abandon their families, leave their wives for a younger woman, buy fancy cars, or turn to anything that will take the turmoil away, even if only temporary. While I did none of the previous, I will never again judge anyone for their missteps. I don't condone them by any means, but now I understand them.

At the point of my crisis, I was leading a staff of close to 400 teacher-coaches with a department of 15,000 student-athletes in a community that loves its sports. Did I mention that it was my hometown and I had tremendous community support? In addition to my own staff and students, I received requests from coaches at other schools to help them in their career on a weekly basis. My job was truly a 24-7, on-call job filled with everything from "the bus didn't show up," to finding a student homeless and living under the stadium bleachers, to a student's mom being murdered.

During my public education career, I dealt with so much crisis that I neglected to see my own issues. Furthermore, I felt I had to fix my own boys' ways to make sure they became "successes" and would follow in their old man's footsteps. My wife also dealt with my corrective prowess, as I was sure that I still could improve her ways after twenty years of marriage. The weight of the world was on my shoulders, and by God, I was the only one who could fix it.

There was so much to do and so much to improve within our program that I became overwhelmed and began to allow myself the very things that I preached to my staff not to do. I told them to overcome obstacles, don't give up, take care of the details, control what you can control and let go what you cannot, shut out negativity, when you hit a wall don't splatter but bounce, etc. I can quote motivational clichés ad nauseam, but I did not take my own advice. The pressure that I placed on myself to improve situations for my staff consumed me. Staff members were praising me for motivational insights that I would post on social media every few days. I would meet complete strangers, and they would tell me that they followed me on social media and would thank me for the messaging. My ego and endorphins from a stranger's compliment or retweet sustained me for a quick few minutes. Little did they know, most of the time the motivational messages were broadcast for me first as I was seeking affirmations to get out of bed daily.

Fairly quickly, I dwelt on negatives instead of all that was positive with our program. I allowed a couple of people to put a damper on my vision for the program and community. I began to give-in instead of fighting for what I knew was right. I became focused on negatives that I had very little or no control over instead of the things that I could control, specifically my attitude and effort. I allowed internal politics to influence me instead of grounded principle and practice. My emotional, spiritual, and physical health were failing. I lost sight of my purpose and allowed my passion for a career that I absolutely loved die. In short, I was burned out. While the external world saw a strong, positive, extroverted, visionary leader, internally, my naturally introverted self was dying. So, I did what I see a lot of people do when it gets tough: I blamed others and quit. I walked away from an award-winning career in a field that I was born to serve. The news caught many of my acquaintances and colleagues by surprise, but my wife and I knew what I had to do. I had to push the reset button.

Fortunately for me, a very good friend of mine offered me a great, executive position in his oil and gas company. He sensed that I needed a change and needed it quickly. Within a two week blur, I was in a completely different career with zero knowledge of what I was doing. My new industry was vastly different from my previous industry. Gone were the politics and negativity that I dealt with in my previous career. Gone were the daily burdens that I placed on myself to fix others. Gone were the expectations of a public figure who was expected to perform as an extrovert. However, there was still something missing and a dark valley left to cross.

On November 3rd, 2017, my mid-career crisis, combined with years of pushing my limits emotionally and physically, caught up to me and launched my health crisis. A viral infection that triggered a full neuromuscular autoimmune response hit me while visiting Sedona, Arizona. There I was, in one of the most beautiful places on Earth with my family, thinking I had the flu combined with an old football hip injury flare up. By the time I got in to see my orthopedic for my hip on November 13, the pain had spread to both legs, and I was running a fever. My wife had to drive me and help me walk into the doctor's office. The next day, after my blood results came back, I was taken to the emergency room and admitted to the hospital for a five-day visit.

The trip from Sedona to the hospital was the ultimate wake-up call. My family and I spent the next three months without a diagnosis. I gave so much blood for testing and had every neuromuscular test known to man, including a muscle biopsy. I had been seen by ten different doctors from neurologists, rheumatologists, infectious disease doctors, and others. Very caring friends and loving family innocently asked me if I'd been tested for Lyme disease so many times that I wanted to punch the next person who asked me. I'm joking of course, but it did get to the point that I ordered my wife to not allow any visitors, and I pretty much went silent by not communicating by phone, text, or social media.

On December 20, my neuromuscular doctor told my wife and I that she was looking for three differentials. One of the differentials was something called paraneoplastic syndrome. I had zero idea what paraneoplastic syndrome was, but when I turned to my wife, who is a veterinarian, and saw her face, I knew it was not good. My wife's facial expression melted me and internally buckled me like I have never been hit. My blood was sent to the Mayo Clinic for testing, and we were told that it could take a month for the results to return.

So, I spent the next few weeks trying to figure out how to increase my life insurance and tie up loose ends all while trying to be the strong, stone-faced, provider for my family. Even though I refused to take most of the opioid prescriptions because of how they made me feel, the doctors had me on so much pain medication and steroids that I lost November and December of 2017. I don't remember much from these months. When the President of the United States talked about checking into the hospital and being released hooked on painkillers, he hit the nail on the head. I did not get hooked on painkillers, but I was taking a ton of medicine. I could not function and definitely could not think clearly.

By God's grace, it took a complete reset, break, and evaluation of myself to realize my true purpose and passion. I also believe that my health crisis was given to me as a way to slow me down and face the reality of my purpose on this planet. The reset also opened my eyes to who my true friends are and taught me to love me for just being me. Even though I had ordered that no visitors come because my pride, depression, and just plain feeling bad (I did not want to allow anyone to see me in the condition I was in), my wife arranged for my best friends of over 30 years to come visit me. My guys, my brothers, dropped everything in their busy lives to come see me and check on me. My wife knew exactly what I needed to feel better when she ignored me and prescribed my brothers to visit me. She is a doctor you know.

I have always known that my family loves me, but my eyes opened to what I missed while I was pushing myself to provide and excel. The blood test results from the Mayo Clinic returned in late January negative. Praise the Lord. My mind immediately shifted from pondering *how long do I have to live* to *how long do I really have to live well*? What can I do to spend the next 47 years free of the stress and the mindset that was ruining me emotionally, spiritually, and physically? What could I do to reflect the love and caring that my friends, family, colleagues, and acquaintances had shown me over my lifetime? What could I do to really live?

I suddenly woke up, and reality hit that our oldest son was a few months away from moving off to college and that our youngest son had grown into a young man. They are both great kids. I woke up to realize that my best friend, personal doctor, spiritual advisor, travel companion, and life partner had been there by my side all along providing love like Jesus and guidance better than any psychologist. My wife doesn't always think I am listening, but I hear her more now because now I know that 99% of the time she is spot-on, even if I don't like what she is saying.

I look back and can see that my move out of my career to work for my friend was providential. It was God's way of making me take a step out on faith to see what really mattered and to find my purpose.

As I reflect back on my public education career, I realize that some of the people who put a damper on my vision and leadership were really blessings in disguise. They helped me to realize my true purpose. My obstacles have once again become opportunities, my critics have become my teachers, and I am focused on what I can control—my attitude and my effort.

As I reflect on the past year of my life, I ponder how many people go through what I have experienced and how many are granted the second chance to find or reignite their purpose on this planet, to passionately pursue their purpose, and to profit emotionally, spiritually, physically, and perhaps financially. Through my mid-career crisis and my health crisis, I have learned to follow my own advice, to control what I can control, and to pursue my purpose in ways that I never dreamed I'd be pursuing.

Email me, and I will share with you the rest of the story....

TWEETABLE
My obstacles have once again become opportunities, my critics have become my teachers, and I am focused on what I can control—my attitude and my effort.

Kevin Ozee is an executive with a successful oil and gas investment company in Irving, TX. In 22 years in public education as a teacher, coach, and administrator. Kevin has successfully applied his lessons from public education and sports to train and lead employees in the corporate world and has made him a sought-after corporate speaker and trainer.

Email Kevin at coachozee@gmail.com.

CHAPTER 14

A Higher Calling

From Broke Minister to Millionaire Real Estate Investor

by Michael Manthei

I t caught me completely by surprise. In an instant, I went from being depressed to joyful for the first time in years. It felt like a thousand-pound weight was suddenly lifted off of me, and the years of drug, alcohol, and tobacco abuse melted away, never to return.

Up until that moment I had little hope for the future. I had started my first business as a senior in high school importing and exporting medicinal herbs (or so they are called today) to support my own use. Thankfully, this all changed the summer after high school when I had a profound and life-changing spiritual experience. I wasn't seeking spirituality in any way, but rather I was consciously avoiding such thoughts, knowing that my conduct and lifestyle choices were anything but spiritually healthy. Yet I will never forget that night or be the same person again.

Through that first experience (and more times than I can count since), I became convinced that there is a real and loving God, Someone who is not afraid to go into ugly places to pull out His beautiful creations, Someone very different from almost all descriptions I had ever heard or seen modeled about "God." Not surprisingly, my passion became to know this Creator, to discover why He'd created *me*, and to commit my life to that purpose.

I began spending hours every day trying to build a relationship with this invisible being. Although at first I wondered if I was wasting my time, eventually I began to hear a loving Voice speaking to me. I decided to start experimenting with what I heard, theorizing that if this really was God, what He told me in prayer would be validated in reality. I had seen people "play church" and I had no interest in pretending to "talk to God."

One of the first times I decided to take a big risk based on what the Voice was telling me came about a year later. In my prayer-meditation time one day I heard, "Quit your job." This was a big step, but I decided to see what would happen. After quitting my job, another morning I heard, "Start your own company." This was the last thing I expected to hear! I had assumed I would just go get another job, especially considering that I had been in my industry for only nine months, had no business experience (herbs not included), and no startup capital. Thankfully I was too ignorant to know how ridiculous it was, so I forged ahead and opened a company in the decorative concrete industry.

The road was certainly not easy, and I was flung head-first into the incredibly hard work of starting a business from scratch. I had no idea that in addition to the 60+ hours of labor per week, there would be an almost equal amount of supportive work such as phone calls, marketing, sales, accounting, hiring, financing, etc., plus the sometimes overwhelming pressure of providing for myself and my four employees. I will never forget the hardships of this first foray into business.

After two and a half years of accelerated business school (as I've come to regard my first company), I felt that it was time to close the business and follow my passion for God into ministry. Although we had turned the corner and were showing great signs of success, I couldn't shake the impression that what I was doing in business was not as *noble* a calling as pursuing ministry full-time. I had often seen ministers being applauded in church as "serving the Lord" or "following the call," but my life as a businessman was never described that way.

I sold my equipment, paid off all my debts, and closed my company. Over the next seven years, I would travel to more than 20 countries on six continents, meet amazing people, and watch God do things that most people would never even believe possible. I ministered to people in all demographics, from those living at Smokey Mountain (the largest garbage dump in Manila, Philippines) to the military personnel stationed in Baghdad, Iraq, to governmental and business leaders from multiple nations. One of my greatest joys was building close friendships with like-hearted leaders, some of whom are known worldwide, and I am honored to have maintained those friendships to this day.

Although my time in ministry drained all the financial resources I had, the season was an investment that has paid me back many times over. The emotional maturity, leadership development, crisis management, and the deep trust in God's faithfulness developed over this time are worth more to me than all the money in the world. While I'm far from done growing, I know that much of the success I now enjoy in life, business, marriage, and my relationships is due to the intense growth I experienced during these years.

A pivotal moment came when I answered the question: was being in ministry *really* more honorable than business?

While running my first company, I was nagged daily by the feeling that if I really loved God I should be in ministry, but years later this lie was exposed for what it is. I became convinced that neither business nor ministry nor any other calling is more or less worthy than another, and that the most powerful and noble thing any of us can do is to fully express the life God has given us to live! I realized I could not honor God by ignoring the passion for business He had placed in me.

Before leaving the ministry, I began reading books about business and real estate investing. The book most responsible for changing my perception of money and wealth was *Rich Dad Poor Dad* by Robert Kiyosaki. Reading this book and understanding its concepts was like waking up in a different universe! It shattered many of my false beliefs about wealth and was the genesis of investing concepts that would soon change my life.

One central idea that leapt off the page was Rich Dad's definition of *financial freedom*: when your passive income meets or exceeds your monthly expenses, you are financially free and can retire. This seed and others were implanted in my mind, lying dormant until conditions were right.

The opportune moment came as I followed the Voice to transition out of full-time ministry and back into business. I moved from New Zealand to Pennsylvania, married the most beautiful and amazing woman I had ever met, and began managing a local decorative concrete company. I left my time in ministry without a penny to my name, but preparation was about to meet opportunity.

My wife and I bought two rental properties in our first two years of marriage, at which time we got the wonderful news that our family would be growing! I began looking for a large enough investment property to replace my wife's income since it was in her heart to stay at home with our children.

We were thrilled when we got a property under contract that produced just enough cash flow to replace her income! But one Saturday night we got a heartbreaking call from our realtor.

"We lost the property," she said.

She explained the loophole in the contract that the sellers had used to cancel it and said, "It's not ethical, but it is legal."

I was devastated. It felt as though the provision for my wife to stay at home was being taken from us. I went to bed that night very upset, confused, and unsure of what to do next.

To my own amazement, I woke up the next morning feeling completely different. I had a strange sensation inside, but one that I had come to know and trust. That day I told both my wife and our realtor, "God is going to use this for our advantage. He has something better for us, watch and see."

The next week, as our realtor and I were looking at other available properties, she looked at her phone and said, "That's interesting...the same seller of the property we lost has put another one on the market."

My reaction was, "I'd be a fool to knowingly deal with people who don't have integrity!" But as soon as the words came out of my mouth, I had a sudden, strange feeling. I stopped. "Hang on, this might be what I knew God would do for us in bringing along something better. Let's take a look at it."

We did not know it at the time, but this ten-unit, mixed-use building would turn out to be one of the best deals we have ever done. We arranged private financing so we could offer cash with no contingencies, which left no room for them to cancel the contract this time around.

As soon as we closed the transaction, we brought our bank in. The building appraised for $150,000 more than we had paid, and the bank gave us enough money to pay off the private loan, put $15,000 in our pocket, and granted us a credit line for $75,000! This changed everything!

Not only did this property produce much more cash flow than the property we lost, but the credit line enabled us to buy several more properties. In addition to this, I learned a strategy that would soon make us millionaires.

We all want a "good return" on our investments, retirement accounts, or savings, but there is much debate about what makes up a "good return." Is 5% good? How about 20%?

Since most people only have access to investments in Wall Street, I'm happy when others tell me that they are getting *any* return. But the powerful lesson this deal introduced to me, which has become a pattern I've repeated over and over since, is an *infinite return*.

An infinite return through real estate investing occurs when you receive all of your initial investment capital back yet continue to own the asset. Since there is no cash investment left in the property, whatever return the property produces is now infinite.

For example, let's say you bought a property with a $50,000 down payment. After all expenses, including your mortgage payment, the property produces $500/month in cash flow, or $6,000/year. You would calculate your cash-on-cash return as follows:

$6,000 cash flow / $50,000 invested = 12% cash-on-cash return

If you either bought the property below market value or increased the value, you may be able to refinance and receive all of your original investment back. Let's say you did this, and the interest rate on your new loan was 5% on a 25-year amortization schedule. Your new payment on the additional $50,000 would be $292/month, reducing your cash flow to $208/month and $2,496/year.

Although you lost over half of your cash flow, you now have your $50,000 back to go and do it again! The math on your return would now be:

$2,496 cash flow / $0 invested = INFINITE RETURN

Repeat this pattern, and you can see how someone could achieve financial freedom in a short period of time.

Is this strategy risky? Absolutely. But with the right team, it is the most powerful and effective tool I know to create financial freedom and to grow your wealth!

Within two years, my wife and I bought more than 50 units and achieved our goal of financial freedom. The seeds that had been planted in me years ago had grown into a fruitful garden that provided shade and food that my family could enjoy for the rest of our lives.

The amount of hard work, struggle, and stress required were significant, but the end result was more than worth it.

As we exited the rat race, it hit me that I had always worked to *survive*, to provide for the necessities of life like food, water, and shelter. My family's financial future was now secure; I didn't ever have to buy another property or go get a job ever again, so what was I going to do with the surging vitality I had inside of me searching for a purpose?

Would I spend my time back in ministry? In leisure? One thing I knew, God had not created me to coast through life in my easy chair. After much time spent contemplating what God had for us, my wife and I realized the simple answer: we loved what we were already doing!

The shift we implemented in our business was, instead of buying all of the good deals ourselves, we would open the opportunities to others who had similar goals and values.

Our investing path is eloquently described in the African proverb: *If you want to go fast, go alone. If you want to go far, go together.* Our journey to financial freedom went faster than we expected, but our vision of the future included a large community of people positively impacting each others' lives.

This led to the creation of our equity management company where we invite friends, family, and other people we know to invest alongside us.

Now when we implement our infinite return strategy, we get to share the rewards with others, and the joy in our partners' faces is much more satisfying than when it was just my wife and I. Imagine this, you get a check back, returning your full investment and yet maintain ownership in the cash flow producing building. The power of real estate investing with a great team can be incredibly exciting and rewarding!

I don't know of any other investment that combines the power of cash flow, appreciation, tax benefits, ease of obtaining high-quality financing, tenants paying off the mortgage, the potential for infinite returns, protection from inflation, and protection from down market cycles like *cash flowing* real estate.

Our team now includes successful investors whose track record spans multiple decades with total projects exceeding $350 million, including my amazing father-in-law Jerry Horst, a contributor in this book.

The lessons I have learned through my journey are priceless to me, and I'd like to share three of them:

1. God will always provide. It may not come in the form or the timing we expect, but He is faithful and worthy of our trust.

2. Hard times are not to be feared or escaped but embraced with confidence, joy, and gratitude. Most of us can look back on hard times and be grateful for how we've changed. But what if we remembered that while going through the hard times? Could we find joy in the process?

3. The most powerful and noble calling for any of us is to fully express the life God has created us to live. It is time to shake off nagging feelings that what is in your heart is less worthy than what is in anyone else's, to let go of regrets from the past and timidity of the future, and to fully *SHINE* as the light you were created to be!

TWEETABLE

It's a lie to believe that business is less noble than ministry. Our highest calling is to passionately express the unique life God gave us!

Michael Manthei owns a real estate investment company focused on infinite returns and is an inspirational speaker on the life-changing power of passive income. His unique background includes founding his first company at age 21 and humanitarian efforts in 20+ countries. Within four years of leaving full-time ministry, Michael and his family achieved financial freedom. Michael lives in Lancaster, PA with his beautiful wife and two daughters. To connect, please email michael@strategicem.com.

CHAPTER 15

How a Change of Mind Propelled this Federal Prosecutor Into a New Life of Purpose and Profit

by Julie Bowen Stern

The truth, to some extent, is we are all products of how we were raised. Ideas and beliefs are placed in our minds at a very early age that form, to a great degree, the person we become. In some cases, that is a good thing and in others, not so good. One thing we all have in common, however, is that if we desire to change the mindsets that control us…we can. Wisdom teaches that we can be "transformed by the renewing of our minds."

My mom raised three daughters and instilled in us at a young age the goal of being financially independent. We were taught the only way to accomplish this was to get a "good education" followed by a "good job." In my family, going to college was as certain as going to sixth grade. The idea of any other pursuit besides the college route followed by a secure job simply was not a thought.

With this in mind, in the ninth grade, I looked at my future and thought I had three options: doctor, lawyer, or businesswoman. Doctor got crossed off quickly because there was no way I could deal with, well, you know, all the gross stuff doctors have to do! As for being a businesswoman, honestly, at 15 years old, I had no idea what that would mean. My father was a stockbroker, and I did not understand his job at all. The idea of owning a business or being an entrepreneur was not a glimmer in my eye. By process of elimination, I decided I would become a lawyer. I knew one thing for certain, I was good at arguing a point!

I attended Loyola Law School in Los Angeles, graduating Cum Laude in 1985. Against great odds, I was hired by the United States Department of Justice (DOJ) as an Honors Attorney in the Criminal Division in

Washington, DC. The Honors Program is highly competitive and the only way to get into the DOJ straight out of law school. Although I had other more lucrative offers from law firms, I opted for a career of service—less money, but an infinitely more rewarding and interesting legal experience. For example, the first time I appeared in court as a newly licensed attorney was before the Fifth Circuit Court of Appeals in New Orleans. I can tell you, as a 28-year-old, first time in any court, to be representing the United States in a criminal case before a three judge panel of the Fifth Circuit was pretty exciting stuff. It was surreal, in fact, sitting in that venerate, ostentatious courtroom at a long counsel table all by myself waiting for the judges to call me to the podium. Many lawyers never have that experience in their entire careers. When it was my turn to stand up and argue, I felt akin to the Scarecrow walking up to the Wizard of Oz! Thankfully, words came out of my mouth, and a few months later the court's decision was in favor of the United States. I won!

That same year, while I was assigned to the Public Integrity Section, I traveled with a seasoned DOJ prosecutor to Atlanta to investigate a serious allegation that a federal district court judge was taking bribes to fix cases. This was a very sensitive case, and we had obtained a court order for a wiretap on an attorney's office, who was also a target of the investigation. This case was life-changing for me, not for the reason that you might imagine but because I met FBI Special Agent (SA) Ron Stern. SA Stern was the administrative agent handling the wiretap, and he became my husband two years later! In the end, the investigation revealed that the federal judge was not taking bribes. We indicted the lawyer and a sleazy private investigator on obstruction of justice charges and both were convicted by a jury. Justice was served!

As you can imagine, there are many stories I could tell about my career and my husband's. That's for another book. Ron was transferred to the Houston Office of the FBI in 1990, and I was hired as an Assistant United States Attorney (AUSA) in Houston. Ron had two children from a prior marriage, and I had the great privilege of raising them along with our son born in 1992. Needless to say, we were BUSY! Our house had two full-time demanding careers and three active children. We were commuting almost two hours a day. Sometimes I look back at it all, and I don't see how we made it. Believe me, there were many, many bumps in the road. I truly credit the Lord Almighty for helping us to make it through without our family crumbling.

Ron retired early from his 25-year career with the FBI in 2007. Because of his entrepreneurial spirit, he never went to work for anyone again. For a number of years Ron managed our youngest son's pop group, Savvy, and then went on to produce 26 episodes of a TV show called *The Wannabes starring Savvy* which successfully aired in over 100 countries, including the United States. That venture is a complete book in itself! While Ron was traveling the world with Savvy and away producing the TV show in Michigan, I was still trading lots of time for money working in Houston as an AUSA. It was a rewarding and challenging career, but after 27 years, I was looking forward to my retirement. But I was not sure when I might be able to do that because we still needed the MONEY!

I knew I did not want to start a law practice of my own after retirement, but I was not sure what else I could do. On Facebook, I was following a friend of ours who was in a network marketing business. He was living quite a fabulous lifestyle: new cars, exotic trips, and what looked like a lot of fun! I said to Ron, "Hey, we could do this!" As fate would have it, we ran into this friend at a party. He explained that he was in the energy business. This intrigued us because he was not selling products, but rather he was helping people save money on life essential services by switching their electricity to the company with which he was affiliated. He explained that for very little money we could buy our own business and get started for ourselves.

After researching the company and making sure it was "legitimate," we were convinced that this might be something that could change our financial future. We were both going to be retired federal employees with pensions, but we wanted more out of life than that amount of money was going to provide. We had some other investments, but this was something we thought might provide us with the ability to have the financial freedom to do all the special things we dreamed of: traveling the world, treating our kids and grandkids to fun things like family vacations, and helping our aging parents and being generous givers at our church and to the poor and needy in the world.

But network marketing? That's kind of embarrassing, right? I mean, we were professionals, and what would our friends and family think if we got involved? Well, I am happy to say we decided to step out and see what we could do. It is all about what you start. We made some money right away, which was very encouraging, and we worked our way up through a few levels. We started this with the idea of what the money could do to change our lifestyle. Residual income is what everyone wants and is a powerful stream of income. We also have received some fabulous perks from our company, like five-star trips to Hawaii, Bermuda, and Jamaica and a new Mercedes-Benz. We have met so many interesting, positive people and have had a blast! However, what I did not expect to receive when we started was the kind of mind-changing personal development that I have gained through our five years of being in this business.

Robert Kiyosaki spoke at the first company convention I attended. I knew of him but had not read any of his books. His message was new for me. He talked about the path I had gone down, expensive education followed by a good job, as not the way to go if you really wanted to build wealth. He advocated strongly, however, that a person should always be educating themselves at the same time they were creating wealth in a number of other ways. Mr. Kiyosaki was a big proponent of network marketing as a place that evened the playing field for everyone. Anyone willing to do the work and learn the skills could reap great benefits for little investment. I could feel myself sinking lower in my chair as his speech continued. It was not because I was ashamed of what I had done, but because my mind had been so closed to the ideas about which he was talking. I had been closed to the idea of creating wealth and legacy in a bigger way. I thought things were just going to be what they were going to be with our pensions and real estate investments. We would be "comfortable" but not able to do a lot of what we dreamed of doing.

I am so thankful now that Ron and I stepped outside of our comfort zone and started our business. Because we did, I was able to retire when I hit my 30-year mark at the end of 2015. The money we were making in our network marketing business made up for what I was leaving behind. And I knew there would be much more money in the future! Although we began this journey to make money, which don't get me wrong, is great and is still a goal, we now have a different purpose for our lives in this business. We understand just how a business like this can truly change lives. We have seen it time and time again. Our prayer is that the Lord will send people to us who want to learn a new way to create financial and time freedom and to improve their lives on so many levels. The hours Ron and I spent over the years away from our families trading time for money was crazy. Life does not have to necessarily be that way. Don't listen to the lies in your head that tell you change is not possible. Just because your life has always been one way, doesn't mean it has to stay that way. If your mindset is "money is hard to get," money will be hard to get. But I am here to tell you that if you transform the way you think and you take action based on your new mindset, you can change the things that hold you back in life and begin anew. It is never too late to change your life.

TWEETABLE

If you transform the way you think and take action based on your new mindset, you can change the things that hold you back in life and begin anew.

Julie Bowen Stern practiced law at the United States Attorney's Office in Houston, Texas for 25 years. Presently, Julie and her husband Ron have their own business with Stream Energy. They love connecting with like-minded people who are open to learning a new way to create financial and time freedom and who have the desire to work to make their dreams a reality. To connect with Julie, please send her an email at contact@Juliebowenstern.biz.

CHAPTER 16

Let's Do This

The Key to Facing My Biggest Fears

by Dr. Harland Merriam

"Raging Bull."

The phone rang. I picked it up and heard those two words. They are an Army alert code for, "You have been called back to active duty." The United States was preparing for war after September 11th. The military would call many Guard and Reserve units to join the fight. I would be among them.

I didn't expect this. The message startled me. I was 52 years old, had completed 30 years as an Army Reserve Chaplain, and was now officially retired. Or so I thought.

I was comfortable in civilian life. I was leading a church in Beaumont, Texas and a few months into my term as president of the local Rotary Club. I had other responsibilities. I didn't need this disruption.

Then the Raging Bull message came, calling me out of military retirement and back to active duty.

I scrambled to prepare for my departure—discussing the call with my wife, informing the congregation, answering boatloads of questions, handing off responsibilities to others, and getting things in order. So much change and so quickly. Over a few hectic days, I brought matters together as best I could.

I packed the car at "o-dark-thirty" (which is Army time for "well before daylight") on Sunday morning, January 20, 2002. My two sons gave me a big hug goodbye. My wife, Barbara, and I embraced, and I backed out of the driveway.

Darkness and fog enveloped me on the road. Darker feelings churned inside of me. I was upset, sad, worried, afraid, stressed. But, I didn't stop to admit this flurry of emotions. I didn't want to deal with them.

My Army job would be to train Chaplains and Chaplain Assistants who were being called up with their units. Unlike these soldiers who would be packing up and heading off to war, I would not likely go into battle. So, I shouldn't have been scared. Sure, I was taking on a huge, serious responsibility, but my life wasn't in danger.

Thoughts swirled in my head. As I headed west on I-10 to report for duty, I tried to repress the real feelings inside of me.

No one else knew I was so upset. Here I was, very experienced as a pastor, with decades of training in the military. Why was I frightened? Why was I so troubled?

Guilt hovered around the fear. I felt guilt for leaving my family, remorse for abandoning my commitments to people back home, and shame that I was even feeling the fear.

The darkness inside grabbed me as I drove in the fog that morning. Tears started dripping down my cheeks. I remember trying to wipe away the tears, push them away, deny their expression. But, I couldn't hold the emotions back any longer.

EMBRACING THE FEELINGS

I took a big deep breath and finally admitted what I was feeling. That was the key—embracing the feelings. Rather than holding them down and wishing they weren't there, I spoke them. In a prayer, I said, "I am sad, God. I'm feeling guilty, God. I'm upset, angry, afraid, God."

That is when I heard it, not an audible voice, but clear as day.

"Let's do this!" It was God speaking to me. I could almost see a twinkle in God's eye and a smile on God's face. I experienced God's ever-wise voice say, "Harland, I have been preparing you all your life for this. Don't be afraid. I will be with you. Now, let's do this." It was that short. That clear.

A peace came over me like I've never felt before in my life, a peace that has not left me to this day. Solid, unshakable confidence.

The circumstances wouldn't change for the better. My family and the other folks back home would have to deal with my absence. Things could go wrong. I expected huge challenges ahead. The fear didn't go away. But, it no longer held me. God gave me peace in the midst of chaos. My mindset changed. My attitude changed. This transformation reached my very core. Trusting God, I became immediately comfortable with the uncomfortable.

Here is the key. Instead of running from tough feelings or hard circumstances, I faced them.

My mistaken belief that I would be braver or stronger by not admitting the feelings was holding me back. By blocking these tough feelings, I blocked myself from hearing that calming inner voice. By owning them, I was able to see new possibilities and begin to write a new chapter of my life's story.

REPORTING FOR DUTY

I arrived at my duty station and walked into Major General Dalby's office with a confident smile on my face and said, "Sir. Your Chaplain is reporting for duty. Let's do this."

After a little catching up with each other, we prayed together, and I stepped into a most transforming adventure.

I didn't deploy overseas to engage in battle like many fellow soldiers, but the next couple of years on active duty were challenging. I experienced a string of thrilling, emotionally draining, and life-building moments. God certainly was with me through it all.

With the motto "Make Ready," our 75th Training Division put our arms around thousands of soldiers in hundreds of units with scores of ministry teams. We met some truly amazing people from all over this country. My section evaluated the strengths and shortcomings of the ministry teams. We helped them build on their strengths and provided training and coaching to fill in the gaps. We guided Chaplains as they thought through their wartime ministry plans. We encouraged them to express their own feelings, build their own confidence, and find their own peace. We prepared them to go to war.

We engaged in deep conversations as their lives were thrust into the turbulence of war. So rich, so real, so powerful. I am glad I was there with them.

The battle overseas began. I remember long, sad processions behind flag-draped caskets, as we honored soldiers who had given their lives in service of our country. I counseled with family after family in grief. One stands out, because of the two red-headed young boys in brand new, dark suits. They and their mom held each other tight as the rifles gave their dad a final salute and the bugler played "Taps."

I have many memories of the hard, but good years back on active duty. God turned an interruption into an opportunity to touch many lives.

Difficult feelings used to have the power to hold me back. Not anymore. These days, I readily admit what I am feeling. I don't like the tough emotions. But, I embrace them anyway. They are what they are, so I accept them. And a door opens each time. Over and over I find that God has another grand adventure ready for me.

DISCOVER NEW PURPOSE

My training mission with the Army ended in 2005. I returned home to Texas to rejoin my family, the church, and the town. For another decade, I served as pastor and remained very active in the life of the community.

And then, another big disruption came. This was a raging bull of my doing. I decided to retire from being a pastor of a congregation. Barbara and I prepared for this change, packed up our home, and moved to Florida. With this major life makeover, I found myself confronted with a new set of scary feelings.

During the four decades of actively serving churches and the military, I had lived with a clear purpose. Every morning I knew who I was. *Now what? Who am I now?*

This threw me up into the air. Where would Barbara and I come down? A whole flurry of emotions again. Fortunately, God had brought me through massive changes before. So, I put into practice what I had learned. I embraced what I was feeling and then started listening.

God is reframing this so-called retirement experience. A door has opened into another, very active and exciting season in my life. I am not "re-tired." I am "re-purposed." Cool.

To my surprise, I am discovering a new identity as a business person. I hadn't ever put together being a pastor and being in business. Now I am discovering a wonderful connection. I can be both. I can use all those ministry skills and gifts which God gave me over the past four decades, but now in the business world.

With a group of very experienced partners in a multi-family investing business, I am creating better communities, one apartment building at a time. I am bringing an array of clear values and the skills of character-based leadership to our business. We make quite a wholesome impact for our residents while producing phenomenal returns for our investors.

I also serve folks as a mentor, trainer, and personal coach. All those years of pastoral experience are helping me walk alongside people so they can achieve breakthroughs in their lives. I bring extensive training and all those years of helping folks with real-life challenges. I help people ask themselves better questions. In practical and profound ways, we work together to draw out the best. I love it.

Other friends my age think I am crazy. I'm coloring outside the lines for sure. But, I know this is what I am supposed to do. I do enjoy continuing to make a positive difference in the lives of others.

A FINAL THOUGHT

When faced with one of life's raging bulls, you and I have a choice. When the mountain in front of us is too tall, we have a choice. When the hard emotions or dramatic changes in life freeze us for a moment, we have a choice.

The key to facing our biggest fears is to embrace them. We will choose to own what we are feeling, allow it, accept it, speak it. And God will keep breaking through in a still, small, and powerful voice.

May God give you peace. May you discover your purpose. May you find the confidence to take a bold step forward.

I pray you will hear the voice which says to you, "Let's do this!"

TWEETABLE
When I embraced my fear, God said, "Let's do this. I've been preparing you all your life for this."

HarlandMerriam.com | AttuneInvestments.com

Dr. Harland Merriam brings decades of experience from serving as a Pastor and Army Chaplain. He and his wife, Barbara, have returned to their hometown in Florida for this next chapter of his life. Harland is an accomplished speaker, CEO of a multi-family investment company, and daylily hybridizer. He continues to impact lives as a mentor, trainer, and personal coach. He wakes up every day with gratitude for God's fresh grace.

CHAPTER 17
Persistence
The Path Through Uncertainty

by Mohsen M. Amin

I have been recreating myself from a very young age. When considering a journey, there always seems to be various challenges that lead to a specific destination. My constant companion as a child was knowing the destination, just not knowing the streets and highways to get there. Along the journey, many challenges, or as I like to call them, bombs, would come my way literally and metaphorically.

Uncertainty of Self

I can remember when I first felt uncertain. It was the Iran/Iraq war and I was about three or four in Tehran with my parents and three sisters. Sirens were going off so loud. We could hear the explosions of bombs, and everyone around me in the small underground room was panicking. I thought I would never see my toys again. Clinging on to my parents for dear life, I had a glimpse of exactly what I never wanted to experience again: that soul-wrenching, mind defeating sense of "what the f**k" uncertainty. It became my life's work to avoid the negative aspects of uncertainty, and it was not until I met it again as an adult that I realized the impact this could have on my legacy. Avoiding uncertainty became the fuel for my drive.

I noticed the sensation in my body caused by that frenemy, uncertainty, in full force again on my first day of 7th grade in Northern California. I felt like a million eyes were staring at me as I was in a full-on suit with a briefcase. That was my attire in school in Iran! They all were pointing and laughing. This was like another stare I became accustomed to as I grew up in Iran; however, the stares there were not of people laughing at me but were of people wanting my attention so that I would give a nod of acknowledgment. My experience in Iran as a student felt like my authentic self. I was sitting in front of the class, playing sports with friends, and making grades to make my parents proud. As a child, managing this job defined success. In America, the suit and briefcase I brought to that first day never saw the light of day again as I slowly transitioned into viewing life as a sociological experiment: I started watching who was doing what and how and when could I model that to get their same or better results.

Getting kicked out of more than one high school is a very undesirable thing to have on your resume, but a very desirable thing amongst girls and teens in my world back then. So, I did that. I was immediately pinned as the bad boy. With an outer shell of utter confidence, it was impossible for me to share my authentic self. And getting "things" I wanted—the girls, the respect, the status, the friends—made it impossible for me to explore the man that was developing inside me, the man who wanted to learn, grow, and laugh until my stomach hurt while enjoying the best things life had to offer. In fact, there were years I would not laugh in public or smile in pictures to make sure I maintained the "hard" image I carried. The crew I "rolled" with at that age handled the area with ease through fear, something I never felt at home with. I always felt like a fraud. Being adopted in by this group set me up to never have a problem getting a date, but always gave me serious issues with grades. I still have no idea how my district allowed me to graduate; I'm convinced it was a group consensus amongst the teachers to just get me out of their lives. Taking classes at the local junior community college was a joke to me and I wasted time smoking, drinking, doing drugs, and chasing girls as these were normal pastimes for those around me. Even though I thought the group was my hand-picked family, I learned they weren't on one unforgettable night.

One night in a club in San Francisco I was caught in between a friend and a gang that was out for revenge. I tried to help my friend and use my status to stop things from escalating. I knew I had a lot of people who respected me at that club that night, and I trusted that they would have my back if an altercation occurred. I was confident. But, no one protected me. The next thing I knew, I had 24 fists and legs attacking me, singling me out. Even the "family" members I thought were my friends ran as fast as they could when they saw me getting beat down with chairs and tables and other objects. Almost every single person stood there and watched as I was being jumped.

What seemed like days later, I woke up in the hospital with my jaw wired shut, having had almost died. My family was crying all around me, scared they would lose me forever. It was this moment when the lack of feeling like myself, my true self, intensified to the point that I'd had enough. During my recovery, I decided to move to Southern California, cutting ties with everything that I knew that led me so far astray from the life I wanted to live. I was blessed that my immigrant parents saw that my life was on the line and agreed to sell their business and move with me to give me familial support through my transition process.

Through persistence, I earned my degree from UC Irvine. It had been a long time since I had actually studied anything (academic that is) and put my brain to good use, but I dove in, stayed persistent, and eventually graduated. I sat in front of the class, I played basketball with my friends, and I graduated with honors. This accomplishment was life-changing as it was an external confirmation that my authentic self could not just survive, but flourish as long as I stayed obsessively focused.

Uncertainty of Future

Even though I graduated from college, my internal conversations around being enough, doing enough, and having enough continued. I've worked since I can remember, and I have always liked the freedom of doing what I want when I want and being able to control my income based on my outcome. I knew that my destination was to be an entrepreneur, because I have always been the one with the lemonade stands and washing neighbors cars. I would hire my friends to do the washing and I went door to door to gain new customers constantly and persistently. Later, I sold lighters and little gadgets at parties. That same entrepreneurial feeling I had when I was a kid would come right out in me as a young adult living in Orange County. I found a job where I worked on basic salary plus commission so I could engage in sales and stand on my own two feet, something my dad instilled in me. I read everything I could get my hands on and began my personal development journey. I was bringing in 98% of the business, so I asked for a raise and was denied. Once I heard that "no," I decided to leave and never get another job working for someone else. I wanted to determine my own future, on my own terms, and create my own destiny. I started looking for opportunities, and one presented itself to me. My gut told me to go for it. I did my basic research and purchased a small, four-seat call center in a city that I couldn't even pronounce or pinpoint on a map. It was a real leap of faith to send money to a foreign country to a lady that I never met (Arcee). I just had a couple heartwarming conversations with her, and it all ended up paying off for me. Not only have both of our lives improved, but I have also gained another sister.

After a few years of showing up as the man I wanted to be, 2008 came around and crushed me. My girlfriend at the time left me when I didn't have any money to spend on her. I felt defeated. Emotionally. Physically. Mentally. Socially. All of my earnings disappeared like they did for so many others, but for me, it seemed like no one was talking about it. I was again on my own in a place of uncertainty.

Since I had started viewing life differently, as an experiment, I decided to include myself in my own observations and try things out differently one more time. I figured there would be no better time to be myself than when I had nothing to lose. After all, it was as uncertain of a time as ever.

In 2011, with the last $500 to my name and a loan of $2,000 from my parents, racks of credit card debt, and a BMW 7 Series waiting to be repossessed, I had to do something. I met my soulmate (Nedda) in 2011, at my absolute lowest. Bomb. The beginning of our relationship was a huge challenge for me, and it completely changed my life for the better. I never thought a bomb could be the best and worst thing at the same time, but yet, there she was in full force coming at me like a Category 5 Typhoon. Typhoons were familiar to me since they hit my call center in Manila quite often, but there was nothing about her I was used to. Everything was a complete surprise. I told her I had nothing, literally, and that I was heading out of the country to live somewhere else and give my life to my dying business that was less than 30 days from shutting down, and she decided to stick by my side.

After meeting her, I left for six months to work on my business, on her birthday, which I will never live down. At the Los Angeles Airport, I bought Brian Tracy's *No Excuses*. I read this book on the flight over and over the next six month period maybe 10 more times at least. It fueled me. I spent the first few months sleeping in spider infested houses only to move into the space I rented for the call center, building a room in the corner for myself. Jeepneys, brightly painted Filipino public transportation repurposed from abandoned World War II Jeeps, were my Everest in the Philippines, and I can't even count the hours I spent riding into towns getting lost until I found my way. At that time, I did not have enough income to pay for my living expenses and the call center's rent, so I combined them and sacrificed myself. What kept me going was that I was being me. I was doing what I thought was right, when I thought to do it, to grow my business and evolve. It was here that I learned that the positive attributes of uncertainty, that it makes you grow, can be a guiding force through business and for entrepreneurs.

With persistence, my income changed every month by just enough to make strides with the center. Eventually, I made a few more calls each day, connected with a few more people, and bought a car in the Philippines, then a building, and then another building. I opened a second center in El Salvador by taking a leap of faith with a guy I only had a couple of phone calls with who I now consider my life-long friend (Gio). All by phone I created a partnership where I was the director and majority owner of a call center in India where I connected with a guy (Vin) whom I have complete trust in. And the most rewarding thing I have done is purchase my parents a house. It was through my love of reading and researching and knowing, that

I was able to find these opportunities and make my thought of expansion a concrete reality. It was not through any phenomenal one-contract miracle, or with a friend's help or with family money, that I grew my company. I did it slowly but surely, one step at a time, my own way at my own pace. For this reason, I know that each success I have is truly a manifestation of my authentic self, showing up to do, be, learn, and grow.

Persistence Overcomes Uncertainty

Bombs hit me along the way—from having employees betray the company (and their contracts) and hospitalizations for E. Coli and Dengue fever, to lawsuits.... Each bomb showed me that scar tissue builds character and adds a unique sense of being a warrior. Asking my soulmate to help me develop my business was a bomb in itself. We had to learn each other not only as lovers but also as business associates. All of our friends and family encouraged us to lead separate careers, but I knew that she was one of those exceptional people with a unique skill set. Ultimately, it was through persistence that we excelled at working as associates. There was nothing hard about it; there was only persistence.

My company has tested my limits for love, patience, confidence, and intelligence on a nearly daily basis. I can say with honesty that though there is never a dull moment, there is also never a moment that I know 100% what an outcome will be. This is the risk I traded for when I decided a 9-5 was not going to ever be me unless I was forced into it through dire necessity. Each moment that I felt like I couldn't make another call or send another email or make another connection, I revisited the adrenaline that lived inside of me from when I was a kid selling baseball cards, pens, cell phones, and anything else I could get my hands on in bulk. The key to business for me has always been sales. Someone will always buy whatever you have as long as you show them they need it and how it will improve them. I realized everyone wants to improve something, and if you can provide them with a tool to do that, most will. How badly does someone need a call center? My life depended on showing people out there they've been blind until being faced with my company.

Over the last couple of years, I have continued to expand and diversify by becoming an investor in a real estate company, a yacht chartering business, and an event planning company. Each business allows me the opportunity to continue to create better, and witness live the results of my persistence. In turn, each continues to add certainty to my net worth, lending a hand to developing a stronger safety net for my own family in the future. I do hope my future child sits in the front row, plays basketball with friends, and gets good grades to make me proud, but more importantly, to be his or her genuine self.

Today, my purest form of pride comes from within but it also comes from knowing I am still at the beginning of my journey. Surrounding myself with people who challenge my brain and add fuel to curiosity and uncertainty means that I have additional resources to help guide my legacy. Knowing innately from an early age what I wanted has been a light in my life, though dim at times and hard to find. My ultimate reoccurring thought has become, "How can I make this better?" which leads me always to my next step and finding the next street to lead me to my destination. When I get there, you'll know.

TWEETABLE

Welcome failure as it is the best learning experience. Staying persistent and taking action obsessively will be the difference between continuing to fail or succeeding. Life happens to you if you are not prepared, but if you are, life happens for you.

Mohsen M. Amin is a energetic, outgoing, optimistic serial entrepreneur and speaker. He has made it a habit to make the best out of any situation and look at life as a never-ending learning experience. He is always asking himself "How can I make it better?" which is his driving force. He loves telling his story and connecting with people and pours life into people he speaks with. If you need to pump life into your team to get excited about life and what they do please contact noexcuses@mohsenMamin.com.

CHAPTER 18

You're Not Dead Yet
How I Transformed My Life and Body At Almost 50

by Jennifer Moran

"You want to do WHAT?" I stared in disbelief at my oldest daughter Maret. "I want to do bikini contests," she said matter-of-factly as she stood in our kitchen and began furiously scrolling through pictures on her phone.

With a little bit of sarcasm (and a whole lot of "Oh hellllll no") in my voice, I folded my arms and fired back, "You mean like some sort of shot girl? In a bar?"

Maret looked up at me like I had two heads.

"NO, Mom," she said, rolling her eyes at me "like this girl."

Maret held her phone right in front of my face and pointed to a picture of a young, lean-but-muscular, blonde girl wearing a sparkly bikini and six-inch, clear acrylic heels. Around her neck hung a huge, Olympic-sized medal, and she was holding a trophy that was almost as big as she was.

Maret put the phone down and began her sales pitch.

"I'm about to graduate, Mom. I won't be playing soccer like I usually do over the summer, and I don't want to gain a bunch of weight right before I go off to 'Bama."

Maret was attending the University of Alabama that fall, and they hold the record for the largest sorority rush in the nation. She would be competing with over 2500 other freshman girls for a coveted spot in one of their sororities, and having gone through sorority rush myself years ago, I completely understood her insecurities.

"This girl goes to my school, and I don't really know her that well," Maret explained. She continued. "One day, during soccer practice, some of the girls were talking about her, so I started following her on Instagram."

I was a little horrified at this statement, as I've always tried to raise my kids to not participate in gossip, but it became apparent that Maret saw through all their negativity. She realized they were only gossiping out of jealousy. She, in fact, admired this girl. Bodybuilder Girl, as they called her, had been a member of Maret's high school dance team but had quit and gained quite a bit of weight. She then hired a personal trainer and began bodybuilding to get in shape. She was bringing a big meal prep cooler bag to school, eating out of containers at lunch, and carrying gallon jugs of water to class, which everyone, of course, thought was weird…at least, until she posted this awe-inspiring picture Maret was displaying. Hot bod. Big trophy. #WINNING. No one was laughing now.

I had no idea, as I stared dumbfounded at that Instagram post, that I was in the middle of a moment that was about to transform my life forever.

TRANSFORMATION INSPIRATION #1: *"Sometimes you will never know the value of a moment until it becomes a memory." – Dr. Seuss*

It wasn't too long afterwards that I found myself sitting in front of Bodybuilder Girl's personal trainer Cody Barta at some little obscure gym in my small town of Friendswood, Texas. I, like all the other moms in town, had always worked out at one of the big health clubs, taking group classes and discussing the latest gossip over long walks on the treadmill. This little gym Maret brought me to was different. It was serious. And yet, here I was, simply to pay this trainer and make sure he wasn't creepy since he'd be working out my 18-year-old daughter.

Cody explained exactly what it would take for Maret to compete in NPC Bikini Bodybuilding. "If you want to compete," Cody explained, "it's gonna take about 16 weeks of contest prep to get you in shape. That means being on a meal plan where you eat every two to three hours, upping your water intake to a gallon a day, working out with weights at least three, maybe four days a week, plus a day of cardio."

We both sat there staring at Cody as we processed what he was saying. It sounded like a lot of hard work, time, and deprivation. A total challenge.

Cody then made a statement that I would later realize is the key to staying the course with almost any goal in life and finishing strong: "It will be a whole lot easier if you have an accountability partner."

TRANSFORMATION INSPIRATION #2: *"Accountability is the glue that ties commitment to the result." – Bob Proctor*

There was a long silence. Suddenly, Maret turned and looked squarely at me. She began sizing me up: 48 years old, 25 pounds overweight, three C-sections, and a recent hysterectomy.

"Well, YOU'RE the #1 income earner in a health and wellness company," she stated flatly as she made little air quotes around "health and wellness" to emphasize her point. "Wouldn't hurt YOU to do it."

WOW. I was floored. She called me out, threw down the gauntlet, challenged me on every level with one sentence.

TRANSFORMATION INSPIRATION #3: *"If you aren't in over your head, how do you know how tall you are?" – T.S. Eliot*

Now I have to let you in on a little secret. I was sitting there, next to my first-born child and in front of this complete stranger at the gym, and, truth be told, my mental state was almost as "out of shape" and weak as my physical state.

After graduating from college, I spent most of my career as a specialty rep and trainer in medical and pharmaceutical sales. In 2005, I somewhat begrudgingly joined a network marketing company in the energy industry. My sponsor, who was my best friend and a fellow sales rep at my biotech company, had encouraged me to join this network marketing company by appealing to something she knew I was passionate about: my church. My church, which was meeting in a school at the time, had just launched a new church building campaign. Soon, what began for me as a little church fundraiser became a full-fledged, home-based business. A little over a year later, I was able to walk away from my pharmaceutical career to be a "flexible mom" at home with my kids. I was with my first networking company for eight years and, through lots of trial, error, and personal growth, I eventually "failed" my way to the top there.

By 2013 I had achieved the top promotion rank in the company, was recognized as the #40 top income earner, had earned my "free" Mercedes-Benz, and was traveling the country speaking, training, and building teams. But my transformational journey from corporate employee to network marketing entrepreneur had taken a personal toll, and when issues arose within my company as well as the energy industry as a whole, I began praying for a new opportunity. My prayer was answered in the form of a new health and wellness company. Like so many times before, I examined this new opportunity utilizing the four criteria I use to evaluate any new business venture: timing, product, compensation plan, and executive team. This time, though, the company not just met but exceeded my expectations. The timing was ground floor, the product was not only proprietary but revolutionary, their lucrative compensation plan was structured for longevity, and four of their five corporate executives had already built billion-dollar companies. The added bonus was the financial backing of billionaire investors as well as legendary athletes. I took a leap of faith and became a founding member of this new start-up. With my former company being a service-based company and this new company being a product-based company, there seemed, at first glance, to be no conflict of interest between the two. Two completely different products in two completely different industry sectors. But, as John Addison, former CEO of Primerica, once said, "at the end of the day, in network marketing, we really all have the same product. That product is hope and opportunity." I soon found out he was right.

TRANSFORMATION INSPIRATION #4: *"It is during our darkest moments that we must focus to see the light." – Aristotle*

The new company took off like a shot. "Hope and opportunity" were everywhere. The pre-launch alone set new records in the network marketing space. My old company had initially given me their blessing, but it wasn't long before that changed. I felt like a target. I believe they saw the comparative success of the new company as competition. My old company suspended me, and sentiments continued to spiral. I then resigned. It felt like a bitter divorce. I had once loved this company like family, and now it was clearly over. Everything that I had built over the past eight years seemed to fall apart almost overnight.

I felt hurt, angry, and betrayed...but I had to keep my eye on the bigger prize. I used the visual of people in my former company treating me poorly and expecting failure from me to fuel me. It was what got me out of bed every morning running "Mach 10 with my hair on fire." It is what fueled me to become my new company's #1 top income earner.

TRANSFORMATION INSPIRATION #5: *"The best revenge is massive success." – Frank Sinatra*

I had always dreamed of "being #1," but I soon realized becoming #1 is the easy part. BEING #1 and STAYING #1 is the hard part. Everyone is watching you. Every little perception of you, both positive and negative is heightened and exaggerated. Even though I'd been physically active and health conscious most of my life, I dealt with the stresses of my newfound success in not-so-healthy ways. I was eating and drinking way too much, not sleeping enough, and taking my frustrations out on anyone and everyone around me. I was overworked, overweight, stressed out, and exhausted. I had the mindset of an eight-year-old. I was pouty and tired and knew something had to change. Even though I knew it would be way out of my comfort zone, I accepted Maret's challenge and jumped in.

TRANSFORMATION INSPIRATION #6: *"Life's challenges aren't supposed to paralyze you. They're supposed to help you discover who you are."* – Bernice Johnson Reagon

On March 22nd, 2015, our bodybuilding contest prep officially began. Maret and I stumbled through our very first Meal Prep Sunday together, grocery shopping, cooking all our food, weighing it, and bagging it into portion sizes. Our trainer Cody had informed us during our initial meeting that it wouldn't be the workouts but the food that would be the hardest part, and we soon found out he was 100% correct! He told me that, at my age and with my sporadic eating schedule, my body's metabolism had basically shut down. "I will send you and Maret a meal plan where you will be eating every two to three hours," he had stated. "You need to get your body on an eating schedule. It stores everything you eat as fat because it doesn't know when it's getting its next meal." I smiled as I remembered my pediatrician's instructions when we brought our first baby home from the hospital. "If you don't get that baby on a schedule, your life will be chaos." My body was in chaos. It didn't trust me. It was time to get this baby on a schedule.

TRANSFORMATION INSPIRATION #7: *"You'll never change your life unless you change something that you do daily. The secret of success is found in your daily routine."* – John C. Maxwell

We soon learned that, just as our trainer had warned us, sticking to a meal plan would be the hardest part. At first, we set reminders on our phones to eat. For two weeks, we felt like we were force-feeding ourselves, but soon our metabolism fired back up, and we didn't need reminders anymore. We would wake up at 6am to pack our food for the day, add my company's hydration product to a gallon jug of water, mix up our pre-workout product in a separate 16 oz. bottle of water, and get ready to hit the gym. We'd arrive about 6:30 to get some warm-up cardio in on the treadmill or stair climber for 10-20 minutes before hitting the weights to work on whatever part of the body was scheduled for that day. Mondays were Leg Day where we worked on our quads, hamstrings, and calf muscles. Tuesday we worked shoulders and triceps. Wednesday was Back Day, and Friday was Buns n' Guns, our intense glutes and biceps workout. Thursday was reserved as a Cardio Day, on which we'd run 2-3 miles, do kickboxing, or run bleachers at the local football stadium. Saturday and Sunday were reserved as Rest Days, although we would occasionally do some light cardio on one of those days.

TRANSFORMATION INSPIRATION #8: *"It's what you learn after you know it all that counts."* – John Wooden

On that note, everything I thought I knew about cardio got turned completely upside down. I learned that, as a 47-year-old, menopausal soccer mom, my usual "endurance cardio" was actually making me fatter. All my daily runs to train for the three half-marathons I had proudly completed were actually eating the lean muscle mass that I so desperately needed. Lean muscle mass boosts resting metabolism which, in turn, basically burns fat as you sleep. As a result, my trainer scheduled me to do "fasted cardio" two Mondays and Fridays, which was no more than 20-30 minutes of high-intensity interval training (HIIT) in the form of sprints on the treadmill or interval training on the StairMaster without eating anything beforehand. As soon as I finished, I would eat a small protein snack and hit the weights. As soon as we finished weight training, we would eat another protein-packed meal. Then we had to eat again at 11am, 2pm, and 5pm. Around 7 or 8pm we'd eat our final, healthy snack for the day. It was GRUELING at first—not the workouts, the food schedule. But, I was surprised that it not only became easier over time, it also became a habit that I couldn't go without.

TRANSFORMATION INSPIRATION #9: *"Thoughts lead to actions, actions lead to habits, and habits lead to results." – Logan Stout, Author of The Grit Factor*

I had started this whole transformational journey with just one goal in mind, to spend time with my daughter. But also realized, that deep down inside, I needed to become a better leader for my young health and wellness company and, to do that, I needed to grow. I needed discipline. I needed consistency. I needed patience. I needed a daily routine. I needed to find my inner "badass" and feel good about myself again. I knew that I couldn't just be the #1 income earner and show what was possible financially, I also needed to show our company, our customers, and our entire industry what was possible physically. It was no longer enough to just "talk the talk." I needed to "walk the walk." As a former pharmaceutical rep, I knew a lot about the "integrative medicine" applications of our proprietary, customized vitamin platform but had no clue when it came to applications for our fitness performance products. Then it happened.

One fateful day, about eight weeks into our training, Cody commented on how well my back and shoulders were developing.

"I think you should compete," he said as he assisted me with lat pull-downs.

"What? Me? Nooooooo." I said in shock, almost losing my grip on the bar above.

I laughed at the thought of me trotting out on stage like a mule at the Kentucky Derby.

"Trust me, Cody. No one wants to see some 48-year-old lady in a sparkly bikini and hooker heels prancing across that stage."

He didn't even crack a smile.

"Jennifer, there are plenty of women your age and older who compete in Masters Bikini."

I tried to continue our workout, but he just kept on talking. "C'mon. I mean, you're not dead yet! There's a famous bikini competitor in her late 70s who's still competing."

Cody whipped out his phone to show me a YouTube documentary by *Prevention Magazine* on Ernestine Shepherd, a 78-year-old bikini bodybuilder. I couldn't believe it. It was a video that turned my whole idea of "too old" upside down. It motivated me to train harder, become more disciplined, trust the process, and keep going on the days I felt like giving up...and, trust me, there were plenty of those.

TRANSFORMATION INSPIRATION #10: *"If you are not willing to learn, no one can help you. If you are determined to learn, no one can stop you."* – *Zig Ziglar*

That conversation and that video of Ernestine Shepherd inspired me. Knowing it wasn't that uncommon for women my age to compete took away any embarrassment I may have had and empowered me to share my entire fitness journey on social media. I put up real, raw posts about the good, the bad, and the ugly of it all, from meal prep, to cheat days, to posing clinics. I documented every struggle and every success. Even though I was training side-by-side with Maret, my Facebook friends and Instagram followers soon joined me as virtual accountability partners. They cheered me on. They asked me questions. They sent me private messages. I quickly realized I was building a huge following of women who were inspired by my journey, and they, in turn, were inspiring me. They opened up and told me stories of their broken lives, broken bodies, and broken hearts. They shared how they no longer felt valuable or beautiful as a "middle-aged" woman. They told me how depressed and alone they felt as their kids grew up, their wrinkles got deeper, and their bodies and marriages fell apart. But they would always end their messages with "...but watching YOU makes me believe in myself again." It blew my mind. As my following grew, I quickly realized that it's our brokenness that connects us. I encouraged them to believe in themselves, find their purpose and live their passion...and it resonated. Not just with them, but also with me. The unexpected gift in all of this was that helping others believe in themselves made me believe in myself. I HAD to conquer that competition stage. Not just for me, my family, my trainer or for my company I loved but for ALL women who no longer believed in themselves, their purpose, or their beauty.

TRANSFORMATION INSPIRATION #11: *"Purpose is the place where your deep gladness meets the world's needs." – Frederick Buechner*

On Saturday, July 11, 2015, seven months to the day of my hysterectomy, I competed for the very first time in Masters 45+ Bikini at NPC's Branch Warren Classic in NRG Arena in Houston, TX. I was 25 pounds lighter, a whole lot leaner, and a completely different person inside and out. The competition was much more fierce than I expected, and I had to keep reminding myself not just why I was there but who I was there for. During contest prep, I saw a quote that said, "I thought about quitting until I remembered who was watching," and I thought about this as I lined up with my masters class backstage. I knew I couldn't quit or walk away. I had come this far and could not let my friends, family, business associates, and social media followers down. I couldn't let my daughter or my other two children down. I had to show them how to be fearless, how to set goals and crush them, how quitting is not an option once you've committed to something.

As a professional speaker and sales trainer, I'm very comfortable on stage, but this was a whole new ballgame. In a rhinestone bikini and sky-high heels with big hair, full makeup, three coats of spray tan and not able to say a word, I was completely out of my comfort zone. Finally, my name and number were called. With my posing routine playing over and over in my head, I stepped out in front of a panel of NPC bodybuilding judges and an arena filled with thousands of screaming fitness fanatics. Front pose, turn, shoulder shrug with a wink, back pose, glance at judges over shoulder, turn again, hit that front pose, sign off, and strut off stage.... Sixteen of the hardest weeks of my life mentally and physically came down to ten whirlwind seconds on stage. When the finalists were announced, my name was called again. From that group of finalists, to my shock and amazement, I made the top 5 and became nationally qualified. While I was overjoyed at making the top 5, I looked at my award and saw that I had placed fifth out of those top 5. Instantly, my competitive nature kicked in, and I vowed to compete one more time. I had to see if I could win first place and perhaps even get my pro card.

A year older at age 49 but with some experience behind me, I took to the stage one more time. It was NPC's "Battle On The Bay" in Corpus Christi, Texas and the day couldn't have been more perfect. Having formerly been only a regional qualifier, "Battle On The Bay" had become a brand-new national qualifier for NPC making the turnout much larger and the competition much stronger...but I was ready.

My initial transformation from "middle-aged" soccer mom to "ageless" bikini competitor had taught me a lot. I was stronger mentally and physically. I was more confident and more relaxed than ever. I had incorporated even more of my health and wellness company's product line to help me maintain my weight, improve my lean muscle mass, stay hydrated, get more sleep, and keep my energy levels up throughout my second contest prep. I was truly in the best shape of my life. That is why, when my name was called as the first place winner for Masters 45+ Bikini that day, I owned it. I reveled in the moment. I felt strong, confident, beautiful, and proud. I did it. I slayed that stage and, most of all, I showed all my fellow "middle-aged soccer moms" that they could do it too. From that point on, I've had women my age (and even older) tell me how my journey inspired them to finally take the lid off their life, to grow, to transform, to take a risk, to make a change, to follow that big, scary dream and, yes, even to compete in bodybuilding competitions. As a result of my amazing physical transformation, my network marketing business with my new health and wellness venture grew EXPONENTIALLY. Even so, the biggest reward wasn't the trophy, the medal, or the money. It was the person I became and the lives of others I was able to transform in the process that was most significant to me.

TRANSFORMATION INSPIRATION #12: *"Once you've tasted significance, success will never satisfy you again." – John C. Maxwell*

TWEETABLE

If you woke up this morning, God has a purpose for you. To find your purpose, follow the path lit up by your passion. Setbacks that you think define you are used by God only to refine you. Purpose is found in these refining moments. Stay the course. Greatness awaits.

Jennifer Moran is the #1 top earner in IDLife, a John Maxwell Certified Speaker, Trainer & Coach, and an NPC Masters Bikini Bodybuilding Champion. A former top pharmaceutical sales rep and trainer, Jennifer brings nearly 30 years of leadership experience to the people she inspires through her speaking, training, and coaching. Jennifer is the wife of 23 years to Sean and mom to three amazing kids, Maret, Michael, and Carys.

281-748-5757

www.GetTheIDLife.com

www.PureJMo.com

PureJMo@gmail.com

www.facebook.com/purejmo

CHAPTER 19

Some Little Things Aren't Little at All

by Roderick Capelo, MD

"Can you please sit here with me? I am scared. I don't want to be alone, and my mom has to leave to go to work."

It was a simple request from a 10-year-old little girl with cancer, but these words would shape the trajectory of my life. She had just been diagnosed with cancer a few days earlier and was admitted to the local children's hospital for further testing and treatment. Within the past few days, her world had been turned upside down. To make matters worse, her mother was gone most nights to work the night shift at her job, and she had to stay at the hospital by herself. I was on call as a third-year medical student and was making my normal evening rounds, checking on all the patients in my care, after the day shift left. When I went by her room, she was lying in her hospital bed...and was all alone.

She asked me to sit with her and keep her company. Being the busy and stressed medical student I was at the time, my first thought was about how much studying I had to do. "I'm sorry, but I have a bunch of reading to do," I replied selfishly.

"Can you bring your book and read in here with me? My mommy went to work, and I don't want to be alone."

After a moment's hesitation, I agreed. I sat in the chair next to her to keep her company. As I sat there reading my pediatric textbook, she fell asleep. It did not seem like a big deal at the time, but the result of my actions was not immediately evident to me.

As I made rounds the next morning and subsequent mornings, it was clear she and I had formed a unique and unspoken bond. She seemed more relaxed around me than did the other pediatric patients I was caring for, nearly all of whom were scared or in pain. Eventually, she was discharged, and she gave me a big hug before she left the hospital. I never saw her again, but her memory has never left me. What I eventually realized, and the lesson that has continued to stay with me, was how a seemingly small act on my part could have such a tremendous and meaningful impact on another person.

It was only much later that I realized the greatest lesson of all: While helping another person has a tremendous impact on them, it has a far greater impact on me.

After that experience on the inpatient pediatric cancer ward at Children's Hospital, I was struck by two epiphanies: I love the innocence, energy, and honesty of children very much, and, helping another person during a difficult or challenging time can have a life-changing and dramatic impact on BOTH of us.

I never forgot about that little girl. In fact, our short time together had such a meaningful impact on me, I began considering a career in pediatrics over my original plan, orthopedic surgery. Could it be that my first love of orthopedic surgery was not my true calling? After careful consideration, I decided to continue my dream of becoming an orthopedic surgeon, but the memory of sitting quietly next to her and comforting her those few evenings stayed with me. In fact, years later as an orthopedic surgery resident, those thoughts and feelings found me again.

During my intensive training as an orthopedic surgery resident, I spent my first two, long years treating adults in the county hospital. I loved learning the musculoskeletal system and treating all types of fractures and injuries, but there was definitely something missing. I did not feel "called" to do this work, and I could not see doing this for the rest of my life. Early in my third year of residency, I discovered what was missing. On my rotation through the orthopedic department of the children's hospital, it hit me like a ton of bricks. I walked in on my first day, and I saw my first patient, a cute, inquisitive, yet nervous, child. In a few short moments, those feelings from many years before came rushing back, and I was reminded of the pure joy and satisfaction of caring for children and their families.

Because of the meteoric impact that experience had on me, I eventually decided on a career in pediatric orthopedic surgery. I co-founded Pediatric Sports & Spine Associates in 2006, an orthopedic surgery practice dedicated to helping children and families. My practice has grown from a fledgling company that made patient appointments on legal pads out of a home office using cell phones to a thriving medical practice right in the heart of Dallas-Fort Worth. Despite market competition from two major pediatric hospital systems in our area, my medical practice has continued to grow and be recognized within our community. How? Because we remember and practice the lesson I learned more than two decades ago...that taking the time to do small but important things has a significant and lasting impact on those around us.

During the course of the last 12 years, I have come to several important realizations. First, there are few things more satisfying to me than helping children and families in my community through difficult health challenges or scary injuries.

It is also clear to me that the business of running a medical practice has changed compared to when I decided to become a doctor over three decades ago. It's not what I expected. When operating a private practice business, our current medical system puts a premium on high patient volumes. This is in stark contrast to my desire to take the time to sit down, slow down, and connect with people, and provide the personalized and compassionate care I would want were I in their shoes.

More recently, another inner conflict has begun percolating inside me. Several years ago my first child was born, and my second child was born two years later. The moment I first saw my children born, I knew I had a new purpose. Since then, the satisfaction of helping my young patients through a scary situation has been overshadowed only by the absolute joy of seeing my own children learn, explore, and grow. It has become increasingly evident that for me to impact my patients' lives as well as provide my family the lifestyle I have always dreamed of, I must spend less time with the lives that matter most to me. That inner conflict has only increased in the past several months with the addition of baby number three!

As I navigate through building a busy medical practice, running a small business, helping raise three wonderful young children, and planning for our financial future, I see the benefit, or more accurately, the necessity of passive or investment income to achieve a sound financial future and to spend less time working and more time with my family. As Jim Rohn once said, "Profits are better than wages." That is no truer than in today's economic climate!

Because medical school provides absolutely no training in how to start or run a business, how to read financial statements, or how to train or lead a team, I have enlisted the help and expertise of many different friends, business colleagues, and consultants. By doing so, I have learned what has proven to be another critical lesson: leveraging the expertise of my network of business colleagues and friends, as well as sprinkling in my own talents, can help all of us achieve a common purpose.

Today, the culmination of my education after medical training has been the realization that there are so many more avenues than I ever thought possible by which I can impact those around me. By adding my unique mix of talents and strengths to that of others, the mutual benefits can be astronomically greater than the sum of our parts. The first time I facilitated the connection between two people that resulted in a positive financial impact for both, I was struck by the enormity of this new ripple effect. Wow! Yet another way to positively change the lives of those around me. It dawned on me that, as much fun as it is helping little Suzy mend her broken arm and helping her through a scary injury, helping Suzy's family reach their financial goals can have a dramatically greater and more impactful ripple effect.

Having been a lifelong student of medicine and many other things, the desire to learn and search for more knowledge is very familiar to me. In addition, I am blessed to know a large number of high-achieving individuals in medicine, business, and now, in real estate. Many of my medical colleagues have come to the realization that our industry has changed dramatically since we first decided to embark down this long, arduous, yet rewarding career path. We find ourselves working longer hours, scheduling more patients and surgeries, and battling with insurance companies more so than we ever dreamed of. We certainly do not feel "rich," although society has labeled us as such. Deep inside, we know that we may need to work much longer than we ever hoped just to achieve our financial goals or have any hope of a fulfilling retirement.

As I began partnering with friends who happen to be very experienced and successful in real estate, I became excited about several different things. First, my financial future is now rooted in real, tangible assets on Main Street, not the whims of Wall Street gamblers. Next, there are the options of several different types of real estate asset classes to choose from, depending on what I am trying to achieve financially. In addition, real estate allows me to take advantage of the magic of depreciation, something every high-income earner, such as a physician, attorney, or entrepreneur needs on their side. Lastly, real estate provides the opportunity for monthly cash flow that is not directly tied to my time spent seeing patients, doing surgery, or running my medical practice. Ultimately, that will free me up to move more quickly toward my higher purpose of helping those around me even faster.

Over the past few years, I have dreamed of practicing medicine pro bono and part-time, thus allowing me to utilize both medicine and real estate investing to continue my life's work of helping children and families through difficult times while keeping me ever-present in my own children's lives. As this dream is assuredly becoming reality, I cannot help but think of how many other friends and medical colleagues I can help by simply sharing what I have learned. Helping others have success in real estate investing may seem like a small thing. However, as I learned many years ago, the small things can have a profound and lasting impact.

TWEETABLE
While helping another person has a tremendous impact on them, it has a far greater impact on me.

*Dr. Roderick Capelo is President and Founder of Pediatric Sports and Spine Associates. He has been named as "Best Doctors" in **D Magazine** four times and was recently named a "Mom-Approved Doctor" by dfwchild.com. He is also a successful real estate investor who is passionate about helping his friends and medical colleagues build wealth through investing in real estate. Connect with Dr. Capelo at roderick@roderickcapelo.com*

CHAPTER 20

From Attorney "Fixer" to Serving, Pushing Through Fear In Faith

by Dugan P. Kelley

Not another dead baby...

I was an attorney responsible for defending physicians accused of malpractice. These were physicians who were high or intoxicated, who had undiagnosed emotional or mental problems, or who simply couldn't hack it anymore. I represented them all and felt like a dirty fixer. I was working for insurance companies and settling dead baby cases for under $10,000 for my clients, and I was dying inside. I knew I couldn't take it anymore, but I was filled with tremendous fear of making a change. Fear of failure. Fear of poverty. Fear of the unknown. I was filled with fear and uncertainty, and I knew I didn't want my purpose or identity to be the "dead-baby fixer."

Unfortunately, this type of fear is something that I have struggled with my entire life. Fear can be a powerful motivator. I hid my feelings of fear from everyone (family, wife, friends, employer, and colleagues). In part, it pushed me to finish high school early. I completed college at 19 and law school at 21. But, fear can be crippling, because it can prevent me from living in the moment, finding any meaningful peace, or appreciating life fully.

It was 2004, and I was having a crisis of conscience. Despite all the success I had enjoyed up to this moment of my life, I was not happy, and I was filled with fear and dread about making a change. One late afternoon I came home early, locked myself in the bathroom, and fell to the floor weeping, crying out to God for help. I was desperate to find purpose that fit with a meaning that made my heart sing. I prayed that the Lord would strip from my heart and mind any vestige of fear and that I would receive Godly counsel from those who knew me best. He answered me. I distinctly felt that I needed to *press through my fear in faith in order to find my purpose*.

I picked myself up off the bathroom floor, grabbed a legal pad, and wrote down my exact fears. Once I finished writing down all my fears without spin or shade, I met with my wife, and then I met with my parents. My notes reminded me to be completely honest. In a series of honest conversations and meetings, my loved ones helped encourage me to leave the security of a job. With great uncertainty, I took a step of faith. I quit.

Since starting as a paperboy at 10, I always had a job. Now, by choice, I was unemployed. I spent three months being unemployed, turning down job opportunities from other similar law firms. During those months, I volunteered at my parent's church in South Central Los Angeles, and simply tried to serve faithfully without a firm idea of my next chapter. During this time of service, I felt the Lord give me the phrase "*serving the voiceless and forgotten is meaningful.*"

During this soul-searching process, my dad, mom, and wife encouraged me to look at switching sides in the law. Instead of being a "fixer," I started looking for a firm that fought for victims, consumers, and entrepreneurs getting started. I took another step of faith. I had no experience working at a firm fighting for victims. Yet, I felt an urge *to get out of my comfort zone, to find true meaning*.

A door opened for me, but the opportunity was several hours from our family, our friends, our comfort zone. I pushed through fear again with faith and joined a law firm that was completely different than anything I had ever done. I literally started over. Pushing through that fear in faith helped ignite a desire to build a law firm that truly serves people rather than our pocketbook.

I wanted to be a part of a firm where *excellence was not a one-time action, it was a state of mind*, where service to clients was paramount. Within two years of making those steps of faith to leave "fixing," we were blessed to have settlements and verdicts for clients in excess of 70 million dollars. That early success fueled my belief that I had done the right thing and served as a fundamental building block for what would later be our own law firm Kelley Clarke, PLLC.

When asked what are the keys to my success, I know immediately how to answer. It always surprises people to know that I don't answer with gifting, experience, or even luck. No, I believe in my heart that my keys to success lie in three basic principles that serve as guideposts in my life:

- Prayer: My faith is key #1 to who I am and guides how I want to serve people. I have had extraordinary grace shown to me over my life, and I want to be able to extend that same amount of grace, friendship, and counsel to those the Lord brings me to serve. Prayer and my faith ignited my passion.

- People: I would not be practicing law in my own firm throughout the United States without having a solid core of people who have poured into me. Leaning on my infrastructure of family and friends is the #2 key that helped me push through fear to find a purpose that was aligned with my passion to help people.

- Persistence: The #3 key to my success lies in my refusal to quit. I really didn't want to leave that bathroom floor many years ago. I wanted to quit and do nothing. I had almost deceived myself into staying in a bubble. Diligent and prolonged persistence drives me internally.

Currently, I'm blessed to represent entrepreneurs, families, individuals, and businesses in helping make a meaningful difference. I don't spend a lot of time looking backward, but I am so thankful for the opportunities I have had. Now, when fear rises within me, I have a peace and confidence of knowing that it is always important to press through fear in faith to find meaning.

TWEETABLE

Everyone has fear. Don't let fear cripple your dreams, your relationships, or your future. Prayer, supporting family and friends, and persistence can overcome any amount of fear.

Dugan P. Kelley is the managing partner Kelley Clarke, PLLC with offices in California and Texas. He completed college as a teenager and law school at 21. In 18 years of law, he has represented clients in transactions, workouts, or structured deals of over $1 billion and obtained over $70 million in verdicts and settlements for clients. From 2008-2016, he was selected as a "Super Lawyer Rising Star" (only 2.5% of attorneys in the country). He specializes in crisis management, real estate, corporate, general counsel, and litigation services for clients. He serves on multiple boards, and his entire family is active in their church and community. www.kelleyclarkelaw.com

CHAPTER 21

Power of the Unexpected Door

How Authenticity Allows Influencers to Walk Through Yours

by Sophia Stavron

What do Billy Zane, Rudy Ruettiger, Jean Houston, and Jack Canfield have in common with me? Yes, perhaps the obvious answer is that I have a friendship with them and that we all have been in films or have produced films. Now for the deeper answer...my path has crossed with each of these extraordinary influencers through leading with my authentic self. Just when I thought we had a common passion for film, I realized that our true connection is our individual calling to make a difference in the world. The experience we all share is the willingness to be our true selves and take action by going through unexpected doors in life.

Do you have a passion or purpose that has been driving you since childhood? I have an undying yearning to help others. It's a whispering from my soul that never quiets until I creatively express wisdom I hold inside to the outside world through film, music, speaking, writing, or one-on-one mentoring sessions with clients. But from where did this wisdom come?

I come from an ancient culture, a wonderful Greek heritage. I belong to a generational line of very strong women, very wise women, the matriarchs that keep the family together. And in that same breath, my father was raised by one of these strong, wise women, Sophia. It's fitting that I am named after my grandmother, and that my name in Greek means, wisdom. Need I say more? Ha!

I have the gift of empathy, and this uncanny ability to feel and see energy. Everything is energy! It is a reality that's not always understood by many. You are like a cell phone. You need to plug into electricity in order to have enough charge on your battery to run your phone. You don't "see" it, but you charge your phone daily anyway...because you "know" your cell phone works if you do!

Reflecting back, it's hard to imagine that I was thrust into consciousness at a very early age. That's my reality! Here's the best way I explain it...it's like having empathy for others but on steroids.

I can easily connect to people's human potential. You know the feeling when you talk to someone that you've never met, but you feel "seen" by them? Or better yet, you feel like this stranger really "knows" you. Early on, I became aware that there was something larger than myself. I could feel people's energy. It's a sense of how they are feeling in that moment. Adults picked up that I did not behave with the usual childlike mind of "the world revolves around me" when I was younger. I was beyond curious to find out what was my purpose! I see and hear my surroundings with such color and flavor! This experience of "knowing" allowed me to connect easily with adults, animals, and nature.

On the flip side, the constant resistance and bullying I received because of my interesting skill set forced me to "toughen up" and realize that I was a bit of an outlier. I smiled, laughed, danced, and lived life with heightened joy to help me cope with other children and adults being uncomfortable around me. I thrived! I learned amazing coping skills on my own through this childhood experience. And because of my life experience, an unexpected door opened for my professional life.

What I didn't have language for as a child, I now understand as an adult.

Philotimo...the Ancient Greek word that is untranslatable in any other language. The Greek word Philotimi ("philo" means *love* and "timi" means *to honor*) has the literal meaning of *love to honor*. The complex meaning of Philotimo put in its simplest form is *doing good*. Elder Paisios of Mount Athos is noted as saying, "Philotimo is that deep-seated awareness in the heart that motivates the good a person does. A Philotimos person is one who conceives and enacts eagerly those things good." This highest Greek virtue, concept, and practice gives a sense of meaning and purpose to life that extends beyond ourselves.

I know and can easily connect to your authentic self. Even more profound is, everyone has the ability to attract unexpected doors into their life...and the first unexpected door is into your inner world. It's what I like to call your inner genius, the core of what makes you authentic.

My philosophy is, the practice of Philotimo can transform any aspect of your life. The energy of love, appreciation, and connecting to others and being "seen" is so powerful. It's Philotimo.

At the height of writing my book and film script about my global Philotimo movement in September 2017, I hit a major writer's block.

Why is this happening?! What is going on?! These thoughts were yelling in my head for a couple of days. At the same time, I also had a mega dose of empathy for the clients who I help daily when they get stuck. It was time for me to take my own medicine. And I did just that!

I said to myself, "I'm creating useless thoughts in my mind, my energy is not focused, and I'm definitely not living in the moment. Get back on your track, Sophia!" When I use the word "track," it's my visual image which I've connected to the word "purpose."

Three weeks from the day I started daily visualization of my affirmations, my much needed answer appeared while I was in Hollywood! The evening started with receiving an award for my executive producer role in the film *The Soul of Success: The Jack Canfield Story*. Immediately following the awards ceremony was the movie premiere event of *Rudy Ruettiger: The Walk On!*, which is another film for which I received an award for my role as executive producer.

Every cell in my body was buzzing with great joy and love after viewing the film for the first time with Rudy and seeing his tears of joy. Honoring his journey! That night I was reminded of my belief birthed in childhood that film and music can powerfully touch and move your spirit and inspire you to action! A wave of realization came over me that my dream to connect with an audience through film, as I've done with my voice and playing violin for most my life, is now real. As I was chatting about my future film projects with my co-executive producer, and celebrating our efforts, my unexpected door opened! I could feel the presence of a powerful energy approach me. I turned my attention to the man who was curious about the two awards I was holding.

Internationally known actor Billy Zane walked through my unexpected door! He's most popularly known for his role as Cal, Rose's fiancé, in the movie *Titanic*. Because I'm a big fan of his, I knew of his great body of work as an actor, producer, and artist.

What is so amazing about how I unexpectedly met Billy Zane, is that it all happened through my daily practice of Philotimo. I didn't know Billy personally before my movie premiere. During our conversation, I shared that I was currently soft launching my global Philotimo WellBeing™ movement. Since he's a fellow Greek, he immediately connected to my vision, and graciously shared his experience of Philotimo with me. The missing piece of my writing I was eager to find during the few weeks before meeting Billy was finally revealed! He unknowingly gave me the insight I was missing to continue writing my book on Philotimo! But I'm not surprised! He embodies Philotimo! Since our initial meeting, we have cultivated a meaningful friendship and conversations of possible future collaboration. I am honored to have Billy Zane by my side on my current project about Philotimo.

Here's the secret in finding your unexpected doors. Your thoughts are like magnets...this is why practicing Philotimo is so powerful. For a simple example, to honor your clients, you can choose to think *How can I serve you?* instead of *What can I sell you?* Energetically you're connecting to your clients on a much deeper level which also ignites trust, a sense of appreciation, and higher probability for referrals. A clear consciousness of service also allows solutions to appear much faster for your clients. And the opportunity for attracting more clients!

Invest some of your daily energy to focus your thoughts on honoring the solution you perhaps are not seeing at the moment.

I'm living my childhood dream, passion, and purpose daily. I teach people how the mind, body, spirit connection is powerful and guide them through their own transformation. Clients come to me for x, y, and z, when really, I guide them through an unexpected door to the results they're searching for.

"Philotimo to the Greek is like breathing. A Greek is not a Greek without it. He might as well not be alive."

– Thales (c. 624 BC – c. 546BC) a Greek philosopher, one of the seven sages of Greece, "the father of science"

It's simple. Live your authenticity in your own life movie! You create your own narrative. Because of my colorful childhood and experience of Philotimo, I learned my lesson early in life to lead with my authentic self and to practice Philotimo even though I might not see where it's guiding me! The results can be unexpected and miraculous! I'm very grateful to be serving people with my gifts by helping them walk through unexpected doors and connecting them to their potential and their purpose. Embrace possibility! I have proof that people who stay open to unexpected doors find beyond them their purpose. My dear friend and mentor, Jean Houston, recently emailed me, "I think that you are a key player in this time of whole system transition." I believe the time is now for you to courageously go through your unexpected doors!

TWEETABLE
Your thoughts are like magnets...this is why practicing Philotimo is so powerful!

Sophia Stavron is a sought-after dynamic international speaker, #1 bestselling author, executive producer of multiple films, one of which has two Emmy Award nominations and a Telly Bronze Award, and an authority on using the Ancient Greek secret to transform any aspect of your life...Philotimo WellBeing™. Seen on ABC, NBC, CBS, FOX, and WFAA-Dallas, TX. To arrange for speaking opportunities, media appearances/interviews, mentoring, or mastermind events, please contact her at www.SophiaStavron.com.

CHAPTER 22

How Being Evicted Helped Me Find My Purpose in Business and Life

by Ken Lundin

t was Thursday, December 8th, 2011. There was a Rudolph the Red-Nosed Reindeer blow-up in the front yard. The "hiss" from the air pump was the first sound I heard each time I opened the front door. Hamburgers were cooking on the stove, and the kids were plopped on the floor in front of the television. It appeared to be just another normal night.

You could say I'd been in sales my whole life. My father was in the Air Force, and I spent my formative years making new friends when we moved every two to three years, and it served me well later in life. I was promoted to Associate Vice President in less than three years in my first job and doubled sales for the company in my second. I had closed $26,000,000 in just nine months and led national sales efforts from under $2 million to over $70 million in four years at another stop in my career. Winning had been all I knew.

When I looked out the front window, I saw two men get out of their black truck and approach the front door cautiously. They each wore a puzzled look on their faces. Their eyes seemed to dart back and forth over the Christmas lights and tidy landscaping. I opened the door to say hello just as my nine-year-old pulled up beside my leg, leaning on me, asking, "Daddy, who is it?"

The men were there to tell me they just purchased our home in an auction on the courthouse steps.

They were surprised we were still in the house.

I was surprised they were standing on my porch.

Weren't we sent a notice?

Why weren't we sent a notice?

Weren't we in the middle of negotiations with the bank?

We were given until January 1st, just three weeks, to move from our house, leave our home, and find a new place for our family. As I looked at my children, my heart was sinking like a rock in a bottomless lake. They trusted me to provide for them. I needed to tell my children their father had failed them, to tell my wife I had failed our family and ruined Christmas forever.

Until that day, it looked like I was living the perfect life. I had my own American dream. I was a business owner with three kids, two dogs, a wife, and a big house. My friends and business associates thought I had everything under control; I was one of the smart ones. We survived the recession, or so it appeared. Now I would have to come clean with my friends, and everyone would know I was a failure.

After buying the business in 2006, I drove the business to be the dominant player in Atlanta and one of the top five franchises in the country out of more than 80. I grew sales by more than 300% over the next eight months, bought more vehicles, invested in more office and warehouse space, spent more on advertising, took on more inventory, re-branded, and had licensing agreements in place up the East coast. It was a rocket ship, and I was the captain.

Then the Great Recession hit and, officially, lasted 19 months. Housing prices plummeted. Access to capital for businesses and consumers tightened drastically. There were fewer customers and less credit available to cover the expansion. Bear Stearns collapsed, and Lehman Brothers filed for bankruptcy shortly thereafter. The government reports say it only lasted 19 months, but it claimed victims for years to come. I was just another name on the tragic list.

As the stress and loneliness of business ownership in this new environment crushed me, I retreated away from my family and friends, away from everything that had driven my success. My purpose had become self-preservation above all else. Survival mode is an interesting experience. I leapt from decision to decision trying to make it one more day or one more week. Self-preservation itself tightened my focus so much that surviving one day at a time made it a foregone conclusion that the business would ultimately die.

I don't believe anyone would say I wasn't passionate about my business. If the volume of my voice, the number of hours I worked, or the chances I took in the final years indicated passion, then I had passion. However, being passionate was like driving a car with no destination. I was going fast, but without any direction.

But on December 8th, I realized the big mistake.... I had mistaken passion for purpose, and it cost me everything. I was driven by my inner issues and external expectations disguised as the hunt for growth and had lost touch with my WHY, my purpose for being, the purpose of my business.

My inner voice was relentless for months to come. It was similar to the feeling of a disappointed parent being in my ear all day every day with questions I could not answer. How could I balance seeking success and serving others? Was business supposed to be a constant tug-of-war between the competing interests of customers, employees, vendors, and family? What is happiness, and how do I achieve it for myself and my family?

Over the coming months, I gained strength as I refused to be a victim of my own thoughts and searched for a way to become a more true and authentic version of myself. I was on a treasure hunt for my true north purpose, a guiding light for my personal and business life.

I believe we all have moments in our life when the universe is moving towards us, and we feel a harmony. As I rolled this thought through my mind over the coming months, I had my first paradigm shift. When you live in a state where all your energy is directed at your purpose, your purpose is fueled by your passion and you feel unstoppable.

I wanted to feel unstoppable and began to look back over the moments, days, and months in my life when I felt the universe moving towards me. In those moments I found three things: my entire life felt right, I made more money, and I advanced my career much faster. Why was that?

> *"You can have everything you want in life if you just help enough people get what they want in life."*
>
> – Zig Ziglar

I saw Zig Ziglar speak in the late 1990s in Phoenix, Arizona. My early career success had a lot to do with that presentation. From being promoted to vice president in my 20s, earning six figures in a single paycheck at 29, and being part of a management team recognized as one of the fastest growing companies in America by *Inc. Magazine* three years in a row, I attribute those successes to what I learned that day.

I reflected on my previous experiences and found my early success was fueled by a purpose of serving others. In review of my life, the moments when I felt fulfilled and made the most money were when I was true to my purpose of serving others and helping them get what they want. When I was helping others achieve their goals, I was closest to achieving mine.

In my journey to discover my purpose, I returned to Zig's advice and realized my purpose had not changed, I had simply lost sight of it. Under the stress of those years, I needed a reminder to stay true to myself. My business lost sight of our reason to exist, which was to serve our customers. I made making money the goal instead of the byproduct of our goal to serve.

Helping others get what they want is my purpose. It is this simple yet powerful idea which served as my true north early in my career. This purpose allowed me to pursue it with passion and without conflict. It transcended all aspects of my life and allowed me to serve others without expectations of a future result. It is the most important concept I have taught while managing employees and advising companies of all sizes since.

As Bob Burg says, "Money is an echo" of value delivered, and your customer gets to decide whether you delivered it. This is the paradigm shift the businesses I serve have made, and it has led to spectacular results for them.

So how well does the purpose to serve first work in the real world?

- I tripled my income in just over two years while being promoted three times by obsessively focusing on serving others above myself and my company.

- I launched my own business and within 120 days interviewed 32 of the top sales influencers in the world for The B2B Sales Summit— including another of my early career idols, Tom Hopkins. We had over 2,700 people attend.

- I doubled the sales for a B2B FinTech company in just 12 months.

- My client increased their average monthly sales by 347% in 75 days.

- Another client achieved 129% of revenue plans.

Helping others get what they want seems absurdly simple, but your 100,000-year-old brain is still wired for the most basic self-preservation and without prompting will choose selfishly to fight it as mine did.

Serving others is the secret to a purpose-driven life which is happier, wealthier, and more meaningful. Your centuries-old brain will fight your efforts to serve others, but it is the path to purpose, passion, and profits in business and life. How will you begin to serve others today while expecting nothing in return?

TWEETABLE

Your 100,000-year-old brain will fight your efforts to serve others, but it is the path to purpose, passion, and profits in business and life.

Ken Lundin disrupts limiting patterns of behavior and uses proven best practices learned over 20+ years growing companies of all types and sizes to unlock sales growth for individuals and companies.

Ken's innovative approach, #sellingh2h, has powered the growth across many industries disrupting the old model of B2B and B2C sales and marketing models.

Connect with Ken and ask how he can help you reach your goals.

LinkedIn or Facebook: Ken Lundin

Twitter: @kglundin

www.kenlundin.com

CHAPTER 23

Expect No Limits and Achieve the Unbelievable

by Udo D. Strick

When I was growing up in Vienna, Austria, life was great. And how could it not be? I was well fed and got to play all day. If I wanted something, I would pursue it. One day when I was five, I asked my father if I could play on the big lawn of the house next door. It was the best and biggest lawn in the entire city (from what I knew) and right next door. My father replied that this was the German ambassador's residence, and I would have to ask him. The next day after breakfast, I walked over to the ambassador's house and rang the doorbell. A lady opened the door and asked how she could assist me. I asked if I could speak with the ambassador, to which she replied that her husband, the ambassador, was at the office and not at home right now. She then asked if she could be of help. I did not think that I could discuss this important matter with anyone but the ambassador himself, so I thanked her and said, "Sorry, but I really need to speak with the ambassador myself."

When the ambassador heard of my visit, he asked my father what I had wanted. I did not get permission, because every kid in the neighborhood would then show up to play, but this experience made it clear that big possibilities can be just a step away.

Some years later we moved to Seattle, Washington. A great new adventure began. I learned English, switched out my dress shirts and pants that I had worn to school in Vienna for casual wear, and aimed to fit in. Even though I was foreign, I made new friends and had a good time, apart from the occasional bullying.

In high school, I can thank my intuition for finding a way to address the bullying. In the cafeteria, a guy that was at least 6'2" and a head taller than me, put his foot on a quarter I had just dropped. Naturally, he was planning on keeping it. I had no clue how to get this big guy's foot off my quarter, but I wanted my quarter, and my intuition took over. A second later, I had put my arm around the guy's waist, used my hip as leverage, and swung him to a spot right behind me. I then picked up my coin. The sudden silence in the cafeteria indicated I had made a statement.

I learned that the right solution for every problem may not always be known, and it may not always be obvious, but it will likely require an open mind to believe in yourself, your talents, and your unlimited potential.

When I was a teenager working a summer job in a factory that cut insulation, I saw an opportunity to make extra money. At the factory, there was lots of scrap insulation that was discarded—in fact, it was part of my job to discard it. I realized that if I could bag that scrap insulation and transport it home, I could offer the landlord my services to insulate the attic and make some extra money.

The plan worked perfectly. For one week I bagged all the insulation instead of discarding it, and by the end of the week, I had it all together. The owner of the factory was happy to get rid of the scrap insulation for free and let me borrow his truck. I brought all the insulation home, installed it in the attic, and managed to make $400 per hour on that job.

I learned that making money can be easy if you are allowed to think outside the box.

That summer at the factory, I also had the good fortune to befriend one of the workers who shared with me his story about buying a house and working on remodeling it with plans to sell it later. I thought my friend was a genius. With the money I had saved in my summer jobs, I had enough for a down payment on a house. A few months later, a day after I turned 18, I had bought my first house. After hundreds of hours of renovation work (Thank you to my parents for helping me!), it was ready and looked magnificent. I rented it out and began to have a monthly income for my time ahead in college.

I learned that good advice can come from unexpected sources.

Back in junior high, when I had told my parents I was bored in school, my dad took quick action and signed me up for the new Matteo Ricci College program at Seattle Preparatory school. The program, which ensured expedited learning, saved me one year in high school and one year in college. At the end of the program, I graduated with a degree in Humanities. Shortly after, I moved back to Germany, to study electrical engineering at the TH Aachen.

Although my studies kept me indoors, my love of sports brought me outdoors. Whenever possible, I played soccer, ran, did handstands, and walked on my hands. One time while doing a handstand, I heard a loud pop in my wrist. I immediately felt pain and got back on my feet. Not long after, I noticed that fluid had built up in my wrist just under the skin. Since the pain didn't go away after a week, I went to see a sports doctor. I waited in the waiting room, hoping the doctor would give me some medicine or soothing therapy. When the doctor became available, I showed him the wrist and explained what had happened. He looked at it for a minute and then said, "I can extract that fluid."

I thought to myself, *That sounds like a good plan. No fluid, no swelling. No swelling, no pain.* I said, "Yes, please go ahead." The doctor got up and seconds later came back with the largest syringe I had ever seen. He put my wrist flat on the table and inserted the needle into the wrist where the fluid build-up was. I thought the procedure was going great until I saw the needle go deeper. Seconds later the doctor had hit the bone and was scraping the needle along the bone extracting the fluid as he proceeded. I was up the wall in pain. When he finally stopped I thanked him, not for doing the procedure, just for stopping. That day I swore to myself that no matter what, I would never ever have this procedure done again. The fluid was gone, but my wrist was not the same for months.

Less than a year later I found myself doing handstands again, when I heard the dreaded, but familiar, pop. I had sworn to myself that I would never go back to that doctor, and so I had to find another way to take care of the problem. I thought about alternative medicines, meditation, praying, anything. My mind was wide open to all possibilities. From the Bible I remembered that to move a mountain you first have to believe the mountain will move when you tell it to. So, if I wanted to have my mountain, the bump, disappear, I would have to first believe that it would. That evening, when I laid down to rest, I began to visualize the bump in my wrist and imagined it getting smaller and smaller until it was completely gone. I did this over and over again for about twenty minutes. During that time, I was fully focused on allowing no other thoughts to enter my mind. At the end, I quietly sank into sleep.

The next morning, the bump was gone. There were no more signs of any fluid in my wrist nor was there any pain.

It became clear to me, that there are fewer limits than I had imagined. In fact, it was the very removal of limitations in my thinking that had opened the door to new possibilities.

This experience profoundly changed my perspective of what is possible and changed my attitude toward things that are deemed or considered impossible.

Several years ago, my wife and I were exploring options for a new home for our family. We knew what we wanted, but despite our best efforts, we could not find a new or existing home that matched our tastes and expectations. On one of our exploration trips, I decided to take a detour and show my wife a neighborhood that I knew was very special with its wonderful, big, green lots and spectacular houses. It was great to drive through the area, and our imagination went wild. We wanted to live there, we just didn't know how. Our wish list didn't match our budget, but that didn't seem to dissipate our desire to make it happen. The next day we found ourselves drawing our dream home on a napkin at a coffee shop, and our vision began to give fuel to our passion. We took classes, surrounded ourselves with experts in construction, designed the house, and became builders in the process. It was an incredible journey with incredible hurdles, non-believers, critics, and sometimes endless work, but we made the seemingly impossible possible. The best part was that the house became a reflection of us, our personalities, interests, and dreams. From two hidden draw-bridges in the 32' living room tower to a large wooden spiral staircase, we transformed our ideas into reality.

When we created our dream home, it was the very removal of limitations in our thinking that ensured our success. It allowed our imagination to spark the passion needed to overcome the challenges to make the impossible possible.

This line of thinking without limits I continued to apply throughout my life and at work. One of these instances was a three-month IT consulting engagement I was offered at a company in The Woodlands, Texas. When I met with the manager of the team, I was informed about the scope of the project and the task at hand. I thanked him and instead of inquiring further about the project, I asked him what his long-term vision was for his team and the services they offer. He hesitantly responded, "I don't know," but then looked around and after a pause described his vision.

When he finished, I said, "I can do that for you."

Surprised, but excited and happy, he replied, "Well then, do that." For the entire time that I was at this company, I stayed on course with my philosophy of not limiting myself. In fact, I took it to the next level and asked my clients to do the same. In meetings, I would ask them what they really wanted if there were no limits. The result was that I only worked on things that bore real value for my clients and the organization. I delivered what they wanted, not what they thought they could ask for. With this philosophy, I turned a three-month contract into a six-year consulting engagement.

In the process of solving a problem, it is not the problem that is the ultimate barrier—it is the way you think about it.

In my work, I have found that it is the change in perspective that most often results in the discovery of a solution or a new path forward.

As Henry Ford once said, "Whether you think you can or whether you think you can't, you're right."

What we think is crucial and what we choose not to think is as well.

To quote Jim Rohn, "Every day stand guard at the door of your mind."

Sometimes our current perspective allows us to only see the world with limitations in all directions. It can cause us to set our sights low and reduce our expectations of what is possible. In the business world, the phenomenon can result in reduced productivity, inefficient operations, and missed opportunities. In our personal life, it can result in unfulfilled dreams, unnecessary struggles, and dissatisfaction. Whether we are looking for success at work or in our personal life, we should aim beyond the expected limits, for only then can we grow and be all we were meant to be. Expect no limits and achieve the unbelievable!

TWEETABLE
Expect no limits and get a step closer to what is possible.

Udo Strick is an accomplished engineer, consultant, speaker, and entrepreneur. Through his approach, he has helped individuals and organizations to attain a new perspective and move beyond apparent limits. To learn more visit https://www.udostrick.com/.

CHAPTER 24

If You Will Through It, You Can Heal Through It

by Emmanuel Bernstein

Growing up on the Southside of Chicago, things were going great until life threw my family a major curveball. In fact, it wasn't a ball at all. It was a boulder.

My mom was 35 years old, mother of four beautiful children from ages 9 to 17. (I was 10 years old). She was wife to my dad. We lost her to the ugly disease of breast cancer which metastasized to her liver. Although my mom was in and out of the hospital for months at a time, she still taught me valuable lessons about life, such as, "Never give up on what matters to you most."

After my mother's death, I saw my dad, now a single parent of four children, struggle with providing for us. I watched my siblings mirror him and become single parents with no college education. My dissatisfaction forced me to commit to helping those I cared for the most, my family. After graduating from college in four years with a double major in biology and chemistry, I was introduced to network marketing. It was here that my mother's words resurfaced.

What mattered to me most was my purpose, or my WHY? The word WHY is an acronym. W=What's, H=Hurting, Y=You. Sometimes out of your pain you can find your purpose. My pain came from all those years of watching my mother become debilitated from her cancer treatments. It came from all those years of watching my dad struggle to make ends meet. It came from all those years of watching my siblings get jobs that would not pay them enough money to provide for their young families.

One Christmas break I was home in Chicago from college. I became a star witness in a case regarding a hit and run accident which took place New Year's Eve. Over 30 people witnessed the same accident, but my friend and I were the only ones courageous enough to come forward with the license plate number from the car that hit her. Repeatedly I drove home from Iowa to appear in court as the witness. The victim, Ms. Kathy, would not get justice if we did not show up. She nearly lost her life crossing that intersection with her daughter a minute before midnight. It was wrong that everyone turned their backs as if they were not there. It was wrong for the 18-year-old young lady to flee the scene of the accident. Finally, after two years, Ms. Kathy won a very large settlement. To celebrate, Ms. Kathy and her attorney picked me up in a limo, took me to the finest five-star restaurant in Chicago, ordered me the largest surf and turf on the planet, and surprised me with a gift, a check for $10,000. It was the first five-figure check I'd ever received. Most people would have thought they had hit the jackpot, but not me. The only people that I thought about was my family. How could they benefit from my gift? I took the entire check the next day, cashed it, and split it four ways between my dad and my three siblings. It was the least I could do for their struggles. This started my journey to helping others with their lack of finances. It was my purpose. It was my WHY. When you can find your WHY, you will find your WAY!

Organo, a healthier gourmet beverage company, provided me with a vehicle to serve others. One of my first mentors from afar was Jim Rohn. He said, "Service to many, leads to greatness." My purpose is to help people become financially independent by changing the way they think and thus changing the way they earn income. Although different from being a doctor who helps people fight cancer, I was helping people. In fact, I was not doing surgery on people's bodies, but I was doing surgery on people's minds.

Out of 100 million people worldwide in direct sales, my mentor, Holton Buggs, became the number one business builder and income earner. He mastered living his purpose. He says we think in pictures, therefore the first key to success is to picture yourself as already being successful. In order to do that, you have to have an image of what that looks like and that helped redefine my purpose.

My first business coach in life was a gentleman by the name of Kelvin "Coach" Collins. He taught me how to believe in the impossible until it becomes possible. I watched him talk for hours each day to people about hope, freedom, and the dream of becoming financially free. My mom's words, Coach Collin's passion, and Mr. Buggs' belief system now provided me with a permanent solution to helping people like my dad, siblings, family, and friends. The dream of one day becoming financially free became a reality.

One weekend when I didn't have to work my corporate sales job, I decided to travel out of state to visit with a couple referred to me from a coworker, Anita. They wanted to be financially free. They wanted me to share my opportunity with them. In doing so, I could see the excitement in their eyes. Chad and Shanita, a sharp young married couple who felt unfulfilled in their careers, like so many other Americans. They saw me as a change agent for them, their family, and their community. I shared the opportunity with them and seven households they referred me too, all in one day. Over 40 people joined me, and more than 20 of them earned a commission paycheck in one day, which was more than what they invested. Seeing more than 20 people earn a few hundred dollars in a weekend from just referring me to others they knew confirmed that what I was doing was right. From then on I spent every weekend for 18 months helping people of all backgrounds earn income part-time. It felt good to help people see a way out from their financial or time constraints.

It was not about me making money, or me graduating in four years from college with two degrees, or me climbing the corporate ladder and having three promotions in four years. It was about me finding a way to help people get out of the "rat race." It became a crusade for me. I fell in love with it. I am still amazed because it never feels like work, and I do it effortlessly. I am like the Energizer Bunny. I never turn off. I never sleep. I have been given the name of "Super E" because if you are around me, I am going to do whatever it takes to inspire you to think differently and live differently.

Success is really predictable. It can be put on autopilot if you know your purpose and fall in love with pursuing it. There are countless dividends called profits that you receive. Profits are like life's greatest gifts. They are the withdrawals you receive from all the positive deposits that you've made into other people's lives. Jim Rohn always used to say, "Set a goal to become a millionaire, but not for the money. Become a millionaire for what it will make of you in the process to obtain the money." When I found my purpose and lit myself on fire with passion and enthusiasm, I found myself becoming more successful by leaving a piece of me in other people's lives. Another profit is becoming a leader of significance and providing value to others. You may leave the room, but you never leave that person. Once you leave their presence, you leave them in a better place than you originally encountered them.

As I look back over my life, I'm grateful that my mom shared that golden nugget with me. "Never give up on what matters to you most." I believe if she were here, she would be proud of me. From working with Coach Collins my first 11 years and now Holton Buggs for the last 10 years, I've enriched so many people's lives. I have climbed to the top in every company I have been a part of. I have built a network of over 100,000 distributors in more that 30 countries and over 1,000,000 customers. I have earned over eight figures in commissions. I have coached several people who have gone on to earn five and six figures a year. I have also mentored more than five people that have earned more than seven figures in commissions. My mission is to produce another 10 seven-figure earners and more than 100 earners producing six figures a year through passive residual income within the next five years.

I'm thankful that I found myself in this great industry of network marketing. I'm even more thankful that I have lost myself in pouring into others lives on a daily basis. People have changed their mindsets, changed how their bodies look and feel, changed their bank accounts, and changed their entire lifestyles. They are dreaming again. Some have been able to upgrade the neighborhoods they live in, the cars they drive, and the places where they vacation. As I share their stories of success with many people each day, I know they share mine as well.

If you are reading this book, I challenge you to find your purpose. When you do, become passionate about it, and share it with the world daily. As a result, there will be many profits you will earn from it, and the profits will be more than just money.

TWEETABLE
When you find you WHY, you will find your WAY!

Emmanuel Bernstein is a network marketing million dollar earner, an internet entrepreneur, a success coach, a mentor, and a speaker on leadership development. Emmanuel retired from corporate America after working eight years for two Fortune 100 companies. Emmanuel coaches, speaks, and trains individuals, groups, and audiences nationally and internationally on health, wealth, and prosperity.

To contact Emmanuel about coaching: EmmanuelBernstein@gmail.com or emmanuelbernstein.com or Facebook: Emmanuel Bernstein

CHAPTER 25

Sparkle into Fire

by Olenka Cullinan

I practically grew up at my mother's wine-making factory. As far back as I can remember, there is the smell and the look of wine streaming through the glass tubes in the production department, the clunking of the dropping bottles, the rumbling of filled up boxes on the conveyor lines. That was a lot of my childhood, that and the loud voice of my mother who managed to conquer the male-dominated product industry constantly screaming decisions over the loud factory setting. She was a part of that factory, which my brother and I lovingly called her "third-child-she-never-had" for 37 years. The same place where she started washing dishes in the lab raised her into one lady boss CEO.

And in all that time, while I did not get to see her enough, since she would often work past my bedtime and leave in the middle of the night to deal with crisis situations, I have never once seen her look at the numbers, profits, or deadlines in her office. Yes, of course, she had a powerful team leading the factory to be the top five in the country with her vision. Yes, she certainly held meetings and held people accountable to their goals. Still, whenever I would spend time in her office, she only proudly displayed two things: pictures that people sent her from different celebrations and events thanking her for the product, and the trophies and certificates the factory won at different wine showcases all over Europe. Once I learned more about business, around the age 14, I was "officially" hired by my mother to serve as the interpreter and translator in many deals, and I dove into the world of entrepreneurship with her. I remember finally asking her that perplexing question: why she never worried about numbers and profits and did not have her goals displayed in the office. Her answer, not so evident to me as a teen, changed the whole trajectory of my own business career and life in the years to come.

"You see, little one," she said (she called me that all through my college years), "while profit, goals, and numbers are important, I never really cared about wine. As a matter of fact, when I was initially hired to wash dishes in the lab, I did not even know that 'dry wine' was a type of wine. I thought it was some type of powder wine that one can put in a cup and add water." (We both still laugh about that one!) "But I have always had a huge passion for people: for making them feel happier, for celebrating with them, for creating memories for them. This passion for people is my life's purpose. I believe in making people's lives better whether they work for me, are my customers, or are in my life. That's how I lead the factory too: the force of my passion fuels the company's purpose and sparks other team members to help us achieve the goals. When I look at these pictures around my office and the prizes we won, those are there to re-ignite my passion, and the profits will come."

That one simple conversation made me realize how important it is to know your passion and purpose in life. I built all my life and my brands on passion from that one conversation. Having no teachers in my family and a very keen business sense due to my mother's influence, I initially held back from starting my own business. I always knew that I wanted to inspire people, but I thought that my ideas were too simple. So instead of business, I went into teaching and was quickly disappointed with the constraints put on me by the system. Passion without purpose can be dangerous for your business. It can ignite you to do a lot of things not worth doing.

You see the purpose inside me was burning not to inspire but to inspire into action.

I realized that simple is enough. Sometimes being the youngest or least experienced in the room is the best way because you don't know all the failures of the world. That's where your "why" will outperform your "what" any given day. Rising Tycoons, my first company, showed me that you can excel in your field to the degree to which you are purpose-driven. I never looked at how much money I could make. My goal was to impact the maximum number of teens and teach them "success skills" for life. We were not calculating profits. Instead, the goal became the purpose: to put 500 teens through the program, then 1000. That's how Rising Tycoons became the "startup on steroids" impacting over 9000 teens and 1500 educators in three and a half years. Just like my mother said, with passion fueling the ideas and purpose lighting up the pathway, profits did come.

I recently read a blog post by Tony Tjan, a venture capitalist, which stated that there are many ways to make a billion dollars: real estate, gaming, retail, technology, or even trust funds. But the most respected business people are the ones who have authentic purpose behind them. While we all strive for profit, which leads to many beautiful freedom opportunities, we spend a lot of our time on the journey there. As a matter of fact, we spend way longer in the state of building than the state of achievement. And you simply cannot have a happy ending to an unhappy journey. That's why your passion and purpose are so important.

What's even more important is to have the bravery to re-define your purpose throughout your life. At any given moment, we are in two states of being: growing or dying. And purpose does change with growth. I certainly learned how purpose changes a hard way: by avoiding acknowledging it all together. My brother, whom I mentioned earlier, is eight years older than me, so I grew up on the cusp between a tomboy and a princess. Being Russian, my parents wanted me to have the traditional upbringing: ballet, piano, and ice skating. Being babysat by my brother who didn't want to do anything with me, and who gladly pawned me off on his friends, gave me opportunities to play guns, war, and to run wild. I actually found it much easier to get along with men for most of my life: my childhood friends due to my brother and the men in the business world due to my mother. This was true until I started noticing a sad reality: whenever I found myself in business settings, the ratio seemed to always prove 90% men to 10% women. I noticed that same issue with Rising Tycoons since we had no girls in our first three academy cohorts. I noticed the same situation in colleges while speaking as a Venture Mentor across the country. I noticed this in my own circle, and I was appalled. I was appalled by my own ignorance and blindness. Being brought up by an entrepreneurial mother, I never gave back to inspire the very millennial women who were…just like me.

I chose to ignore that purpose for a long time because I did not even know what it was like to have a tribe of women around me. Men were in my surroundings. I grew up with them, and that was easy.

It all changed with being a part of the *Passionistas* book. Meeting incredible women from all over the country who are living out their passion and purpose made me face how much I missed female connection. Getting raw and real here, I was horrified because, while I knew that I wanted to see more badass women and that I had capability and trainings to make that happen, I had fear and doubts that I could never work with women on my own. Yea. Seems crazy, I know.

I actually distinctly remember having a conversation with *Millennial Magazine* and them asking me if I wanted to inspire more millennial women to build their dreams. (Cue me fainting slowly on the inside.)

But you see, you cannot ignore your purpose forever, and surprisingly, it was one of my closest guy friends who sat me down and said, "Stop being a scared chick. You gotta go and inspire more badass women just like you!" The irony, I know. But that's the true story of how #iStartFirst brand was born, from just one simple hashtag to show women that if you want to pursue your passion—you have to start first.

I remember the very first boot camp that I ran in Phoenix, AZ. I was reluctant to market this event because I was fearful that I could not share my purpose with women just like me and never worked with groups of only women before. I actually allowed one man in (haha, I know, insert eye roll), and ended up with the first 20 women who took a chance on me while I was transforming their thinking and businesses. Today, #iStartFirst Bossbabes Bootcamps take place online and inspires women from all states and countries. This program inspires them into action, to start first. They lovingly named themselves, "the Sparkle Tribe," which was born out of the very first feedback given to me by one of the women after the first boot camp. She wrote, "Being in this tribe feels like sitting around the fire and watching sparkles from the flames go up in the sky. We are the sparkles. Every single one of us." I still get goosies when I read that. But having these women jumping "off the ledge" with me monthly, having my back, growing with me, taking chances, and ignoring doubts is what turned my passion into purpose and profits. It turned my sparkle into fire. And the old adage goes, "She who leaves a little sparkle everywhere she goes can never be forgotten."

You need to learn to trust your gut and you will surpass your own expectations. True passion comes with tears, laughter, help, gratitude, and confidence. Whatever you do, create your vibe. Find your tribe, the ones who are ready to jump "off the ledge" with you, the ones who have your back so you can too walk through your doubts and turn your passion into purpose and profits.

TWEETABLE
You simply cannot have a happy ending to an unhappy journey.

Olenka Cullinan, is a speaker, founder of #iStartFirst, Amazon bestselling author, and Bossbabes success coach. Olenka has developed a "Backbone of Success"™ method that helps women leaders to up-level their business and mindset. Her work as a startup venture mentor, combined with humor and personal experiences, led to her two TEDx talks, Phoenix Business Journal 40Under40class of 2017, global exposure, and her becoming one of the premier consultants. You can reach her on social media via Instagram, Facebook, or Twitter: @olenkacullinan

Website: https://www.olenkacullinan.com

CHAPTER 26

From Employee to Business Owner
Learning to Fight On Past My Fear

by John Bogdanov

"If you want to start a business, figure out how to help someone else."

I t is a simple concept to understand, but not an easy concept to implement. On the first day of classes in USC's Lloyd Greif Center for Entrepreneurial Studies, Tom O'Malia told us, "If you want to start a business, figure out how to help someone else." And ever since that day, I have known that is what I want to do with my life.

Once I graduated, I took a regular day job, as I didn't think I was actually ready to start a business and solve someone else's problem. But I told myself I would look for opportunities to get started. When that company started to experience major financial difficulties, I was laid off. A month later, it closed its doors. At this point, I was hit with a double whammy. First, I had been let go, which was a new and harsh experience. Second, the company for which I had worked failed. This left me with a lot of questions. What had I done wrong? Should I have done more research on the company? Should I have seen the financial trouble coming? What did the failure say about me? Where would I and where should I go from there?

Growing up, I lived a reasonably comfortable life. I did well in school. I was never in any real trouble. I was good in sports. Aside from some minor bullying that pretty much every kid endures, I had it pretty easy. I had not experienced any major "failures," so losing my first job with a company that would eventually fail was a big deal for me.

For the first time in my life, I realized I didn't have all the answers, and I wasn't quite sure what to do. But looking back, knowing what I know now, the worst part was that I didn't know I needed to ask for help. Even more so, I didn't really know how to ask for help. When you have always had the answer or have been able to figure it out on your own, you start thinking that is how it is always supposed to be. Or at least, I did.

While I was unemployed, I read *Rich Dad Poor Dad* by Robert Kiyosaki on the recommendation of my parents. It started to change my thinking, but I still had a long way to go.

As I started a new job, I continued to look for opportunities to start a business. I quickly realized that I did not like my new job but also felt that I needed to keep it for the paycheck. Soon enough, the paycheck wasn't worth the frustration. That frustration started pushing me to focus more on finding business opportunities.

While I had some great ideas, they always became overwhelming. Each idea that seemed so great initially would be met with several reasons why it might not work. My excitement and enthusiasm always gave way to fear.

Over the years, I moved to other jobs just as frustrating as the last, and even soul-crushing. Along the way, I made a couple of feeble attempts at starting other businesses. I also closed myself off from many more opportunities as I allowed fear to run the show.

It wasn't until a visit to a doctor that things really changed. It was my first time seeing my new doctor. Within a few minutes of chatting with me, she told me that physically I was fairly healthy. However, mentally and emotionally, I needed to make some changes. In those first few minutes of conversation, she was able to understand that I felt unfulfilled and was very frustrated with my current situation. As an aspiring entrepreneur, I was failing. She told me I needed to leave my current job and start doing what I really wanted to be doing. My job was slowing killing me.

It was really tough to hear, but also made all the sense in the world. Of course, I needed to stop working a regular day job. I had always known it, but I had been too afraid to do anything about it.

What I should have done was turn in my resignation the next day. But, of course, I didn't. Even though I knew I needed to leave, I was still too afraid to take that leap. So I continued on, but with a new focus on finding that opportunity.

One day, that opportunity came in a vague email from Jesus Arriaga, a friend of my dad's. He said he had an opportunity that I could work on the side. If I were interested, he would be happy to get together to discuss the details. This time I did not close down or even hesitate. I jumped on it.

The opportunity turned out to be a position under the new company he had started, Telworx Inc. I would work as an independent contractor selling telecommunications services, acting as the middleman, or broker, between small businesses and the service providers. It was a great opportunity, and I took advantage of it. I could not wait to get started. It was going to be so fulfilling to help small businesses and entrepreneurs just like me. I would allow them to focus on their businesses while I found the best services for them.

But then a funny thing happened. It turned out fear was still playing its game, and it did not want to lose. Thoughts started creeping into my head. *What if I fail? What if I get more business than I can handle? What if I get a business with needs I can't meet? What if....*

It was the same pattern beginning to emerge, or more accurately, almost the same pattern. In years past, I would have crumbled under the weight of the fear. I would have put my head down and taken myself out of the game. But through all of the frustration and failed attempts, something had started to change—me. I was starting to become a different person. The seeds first planted at Lloyd Greif Center for Entrepreneurial Studies, watered by books like *Rich Dad Poor Dad* and various podcasts, were starting to bear their fruit. The wisdom and guidance from mentors had started to sink in and encourage me. Fear kept throwing its same junk, but I had started learning how to hit that curveball. It was not easy, and it took some time, but I started to fight my way beyond the fear.

The next opportunity came when my dad and I attended Gene Guarino's Residential Assisted Living Academy. As a family, we had decided we wanted to start a business. When we discovered residential assisted living and the training offered by Gene, we knew it was the direction we wanted to take. A business where, as Gene says, you can do good and do well fit exactly what I wanted to do as an entrepreneur and what our family wanted to do as well. We initially came home from Phoenix all fired up and ready to go. But just like any other training or conference, it doesn't take long for the excitement to fade and the weight of the "real world" to start beating you back into your old routines. While we had looked at a few homes in our area and started talking to a few people, we were not pursuing it with our full force or energy.

The breakthrough for me finally came during the first family vacation we had taken since I had been in high school. We were in Northern California's Mammoth Mountain, enjoying the week between Christmas and New Years skiing and snowboarding. One morning midway through the week, I woke up early, before anyone else. Sitting alone with my thoughts, I realized I wanted to be able to take more trips like this one. I wanted the freedom to spend more time with family and friends. I was finally done working to fulfill the dreams of others. Instead of focusing on all of the "what ifs," it was time to start focusing on "How can I?" It was time to start fulfilling my dreams. It was time to start fighting back against fear.

When I got home, I went to work. While I was not yet ready to leave my day job, I started spending nights and weekends working to build my businesses. I began attending networking events. I started surrounding myself with different people. I didn't cut my old friends out of my life, but I was spending less time with them. I began to hang around people who had done the things I wanted to do. I pushed myself out of my familiar comfort zones. I moved away from the negative people who were going to point out all the reasons I might fail and how terrible it would be if I did. I moved toward people who encouraged me, who told me that even if I did fail, it was not the end of the world. It would just be an event from which I would learn so that I would succeed the next time.

The day finally came when enough was enough. It was toward the end of my requisite week's vacation from the day job. I was having breakfast with my parents, discussing our business plans and what our next steps might be. We were in the process of acquiring our first residential assisted living home which already had a positive cash flow. I was neglecting my business with Telworx Inc. So I asked, "*Why should I continue working for someone else, minding their business, while I neglect my own?*" That morning, I realized it was time to make the big leap and finally leave the day job behind for good.

My first morning back from vacation, I went directly to my boss and asked if we could chat with her boss. Thankfully they were both available. I had to do it fast, like ripping off that old proverbial band-aid. Going into it, fear was screaming at the top of its lungs for me to stop, to turn back. But I fought through it. I moved forward with my decision and turned in my resignation. And once I did, the fear disappeared. It was replaced by a calm, peaceful relief.

Over the next couple of weeks, the reality of my decision started to settle. I was experiencing all of those, "for the last time" moments. But even more so, I was able to look forward with new excitement and enthusiasm. I had taken a massive step toward achieving my dreams.

Today, I have the freedom to spend time with family and friends. I have built businesses in which I am solving problems, helping, and serving people. I have taken on additional mentors like Kyle Wilson and The Real Estate Guys, Robert Helms and Russell Gray. And as I continue to move forward, more doors open, more opportunities become available. All in all, my life has changed significantly.

Through all of the changes though, one constant remains: fear. Fear has not gone away, and I doubt that it ever will. But I am alright with that. I have learned that there is nothing wrong with being afraid. In fact, all of those failed attempts and missed opportunities have taught me to embrace fear, because it means that an incredible opportunity is coming. But, even understanding that, I still struggle to deal with fear. In fact, I have struggled to tell you my story because of fear. But knowing that I might be able to help just one person with my story was enough motivation for me to fight through that fear. At USC, our fight song is "Fight On!" And that is what I do when fear creeps back into the picture. I recognize it for what it is and Fight On!

TWEETABLE
All of those failed attempts and missed opportunities have taught me to embrace fear because it means that an incredible opportunity is coming.

John Bogdanov is an entrepreneur, investor, and educator. His journey has taken him from frustrated employee to thriving entrepreneur, with multiple ventures focused on helping and serving others. Whether providing clean, safe, and dignified housing for the elderly, helping businesses with their telecommunications needs, or helping investors earn substantial returns, he is dedicated to enriching the lives of all of those around him. Send John an email at fighton@blackalderinc.com.

CHAPTER 27

From the Dark Side to the Light

How I Turned My Pain into Power and Found My Purpose

by Andre Paradis

don't know how many can relate to this, but did you ever have the feeling of being completely alone in the world? I know that feeling. Have any of you had the same feeling even when surrounded with people? I know that feeling too.

My story started before I was born. I was born in Montreal. My family is Catholic. One of the funny things about Catholics, there are very few things funny about Catholics, but one thing is, Catholics don't believe in contraceptives and they love to drink wine. I was a product of a wine-induced evening so...you guessed it. I was an accident!

By then my mother had three kids, all planned well. And unlike most women, my mother was sick for the entire nine months with each one of us. Since I was unplanned and unexpected, being sick for nine months while building their new house, amongst other things, was not in good timing. My mother resented the pregnancy, and in turn, resented me. I was born knowing this in my bones. "I don't want you here!" turned into "We don't want you here." in my mind.

This was confusing and hurtful all at once.

I was born with a giant hole in my heart, which I was never without and which I was always conscious of. I was five years old when I put the words to my feelings "You don't belong here. These are not your people. They don't like you, and you don't like them. You're on your own." Wow, harsh!

In that moment, I realized that was completely alone in the world and that I was only able to count on me from here on. I was alone, abandoned, rejected, and scared. I knew in that moment that I would have to fend for myself. No one would help or protect me. It was terrifying for a five-year-old, but this was my reality.

Somehow I managed well enough. I didn't care much about anything, understandably. I did poorly in school. I was a loner, awkward, and I learned to compulsively watch everything and everyone around me. Part of it was looking for a reason for my demise, and part of it was looking for meaning for my life and my circumstances. I was looking for a reason to be here. I was looking for a reason to stay here. Yep, I was on the edge of suicide all the way through.

Let's fast forward to high school. I went to a private school with an extensive physical education program. In the beginning of my first year, a pretty, young woman asked me to sign up with her for ballroom dancing lessons, a part of the school PE program. She was cute. She was super cute. So, of course, I said yes!

Somehow, having never taken a dance class in my life, this felt natural to me and my body. I could copy everything the teacher showed us. I could feel it and reproduce the steps instantly. Huh! Interesting.

Not only did I have a knack for this, I loved the feeling of the music and my body vibrating together at the same time. It was amazing. I believe that I smiled, truly for the first time in my life, that day. This feeling lit up my soul. I felt joy and a light-heartedness within instead of dread and sadness like I had every other day of my life.

Then I noticed that women love a man who can dance, so...I made it my career. I became a dancer.

I started training, and training, and training, and quickly, within a couple of years, I was competitive and able to book work. However, I couldn't book a job to save my life! I had it. I knew I had it. But somehow, I couldn't connect. I couldn't book.

I was broke. This was getting me nowhere, so eventually, I decided to quit. I didn't know what else I was going to do, but this wasn't working. Later that month, a friend of mine called from Los Angeles. He wanted me to come help him with his dance demo reel. Okay! I came down to Los Angeles with my girlfriend. We were taking a vacation and helping my friend.

Two days after we arrived, there was a party in the studio we were rehearsing in. There were hundreds of people there that night. I was having fun dancing with my girl. I was partying in LA. But then, I noticed an older gentleman in the corner watching me. I didn't care; I kept partying with my girl. But every time I looked to my left, he was watching me, and watching me.... What the…?

Then I remember thinking, "Oh...we're in Hollywood. I get it."

A second later, this man was right next to me. He said, "You're a great dancer!"

I replied, "Huh! Thank you?" not knowing what the hell he was going to say, but expecting something weird.

He said, "Listen, I choreograph for a world-famous show. Four months ago I lost one of my dancers. I can't find anyone in town to replace him. You are exactly what I'm looking for.... Are you interested?

In my mind rang, "Wait…what?" This was not what I expected to hear. I was trying to process this for a moment, then I blurted out the obvious question, "What's the show?"

He said proudly, "I choreograph for the world-famous Men of Chippendales Revue."

I remember thinking, "A strip show? He wants me to be a stripper? "Hell no! I'm a professionally-trained commercial dancer! I'm no stripper. However, no one was paying me to do that!" I was broke, and this was some validation for my talents. (I guess!)

So...I said yes. Little did I know, this moment was going to change the course of my life completely and forever.

Two weeks later, I was getting ready to go on for my first night on stage. All of a sudden, I felt that something was really wrong. I was embarrassed, humiliated. I felt weird and cheap. I was thinking, "I'm not this guy!"

And I wasn't one of those guys. All I wanted to do was run out the back door. But I couldn't. I needed this job. I needed this money. But it was all so wrong. How did I get myself in this mess? I was next...a bit late for rethinking my choices. "I'm trapped!"

The last guy finished. A ground shaking roar from the audience of 2000 women followed. Then, blackout. My turn.

"Shit! I don't want to do this!" I really didn't want to do this. I was frozen. Time stopped.

Now what?

Suddenly a voice came over me: gentle, warm, and reassuring. "It's okay. It's okay. This is good. It's a means to…. This is a path to something bigger. Just go!

I unfroze instantly, relaxed into my body, and I went. The music started, and, oh wow! I have to say, at this point, that was the best day of my life! The screams, the energy, the look on their faces. It was unbelievable.

The guy who blended in everywhere was now buried by the screams of thousands of women. It was fantastic! This was a pivotal moment for me. It flipped a switch inside me, and in a magical way…the light came on. The only way to describe it is to say that "it brought me back to life."

For the other guys, that energy went to their heads. For me, it went to my heart. It filled me up inside. It was beautiful, and it shifted something deep inside me. Forever.

The show went on twice a night, five days a week, with an average on 4000 women per night. It was so much fun! I didn't want to do anything else.

However, a year plus into this, I realized how dangerous this job was for me. I always saw myself as a professional athlete. Dancing professionally requires great focus and constant training to stay on point and competitive.

At that point, I hadn't trained for more than a year. Life on the road was sex, drugs, Rock and Roll, alcohol, and women every day! It was fun, but it was really getting me nowhere and was destructive to my body, the very thing that sustained my life. I had to get back to my life. I had to get back to me. So, I quit. I flew back to Los Angeles where I was unemployed again. This time on purpose!.

Shortly after I settled in, I got a call from my agent. There was an audition for a job with Michael Jackson. Oh man! "I'm out of shape, I'll probably embarrass myself," I'm thinking, "but, screw it. I'm going just to be part of something like that!"

I showed up with low confidence and high awareness of the scope of what I was getting into. This was a cattle call, which means that the agencies had literally broadcasted the audition everywhere. 1100 dancers showed up… and me!

They would bring us in the studio in groups of 20, put us through a dance routine, then proceed in eliminating people for the next four days. The first day, half the dancers when home. It was the same thing on day two and day three. On day four, amazingly, I was still standing. That last day was like a marathon boot camp from hell.

They put us through everything, every style of dance: jazz, modern, couples, contemporary, freestyle, and solos. At one point they even had us in groups of similar body types, sorting through and eliminating people. And...I was still standing. About 60 of us went home at the end of day four. We were dismissed with the classic phrase, "Thank you for your hard work. We'll make our final decision and will let your agents know. Good day!" I went home feeling pretty good. I showed up and made it to the end. I also knew that it meant nothing at all. They needed 12 men only.

It was late afternoon. I went and had a bite to eat. I ran some errands. When I got home, the light was flashing on my answering machine, as usual. The last message (from my agent) said, "Hi Andre, it's Theresa. I wanted to say congratulations, you booked the job with Michael. Rehearsal starts in two weeks, I'll be sending your contract...." I heard nothing else, because I was screaming my lungs out. I got the job! What!? Michael Jackson wants me? The guy no one ever wants, the guy no one ever sees, is wanted by Michael Jackson?

I finally was in line with my purpose, and I was ON! "What a ride," I thought. "What it took to get here....Phew!" This was it! The beginning of me, and my legacy, and my life! I was on track. I had arrived. Michael was amazing, kind, sweet, and shy, exactly what he seems to be on TV.

Two months later, I auditioned for Prince. I got the job!

Six months after that, I auditioned for Paula Abdul. I got the job!

What had happened was that I had reconnected to my spirit. I'm living my purpose, and people can feel it. They can feel me. The love that I have for me and the fact that I am "full" they can see and is what they connect to. Everything was different. I am fully present, authentic, radiating joy, and people are attracted to that.

I had a dancing career for over 15 years. I traveled the world. I got paid. It was fantastic! I found my way and lived my life's purpose. However, my biggest accomplishment, the biggest gift of all, was finding my beautiful wife, Nancy.

I came full circle, you see. My pain gave me strength. My strength helped me push through to my passion. My passion lit up my heart which got me to my life! I went after my life, and it gave me the joy and inspiration to constantly seek fulfillment. Geez! That's pretty good.

Today, my life is about helping people do what I did. I turned my pain into power and inspiration. You see, when your pain doesn't kill you, and you don't succumb to addictions to numb your soul, your pain is your greatest source of power and inspiration. It is the juice that gets your life to be what it's supposed to be. No mistake! I understand that now. I wasn't a mistake. All of us are on a mission of our own. Some are more obvious, some we have to dig out, but I promise, your mission is in there. No one was ever born randomly. You feel me?

Life is not easy, and it's not supposed to be easy. It's what you do with your circumstances that matters. You can let your circumstances kill you or build you up. It is entirely up to you. Your circumstances are like manure. Manure stinks and is toxic to humans. However, use it as fertilizer and God knows what beautiful things you can grow.

You choose.

Andre Paradis

TWEETABLE

Your pain is your greatest source of Power and Inspiration. This gift of struggle is exactly the juice you need to get your life to what it's supposed to be in Love, Life, Relationships, and Business

#Livingyourpurpose #personalpower #Livingthedream

Andre works with Men and Women of all orientations and helps them find, build, and sustain healthy, loving, and fulfilling long-time relationships.

Often, relationships can seem to be a power struggle, and that's exactly the point. The magic is to be fully aware of the energy mechanism in place in these dynamics and learn to negotiate your wants and needs to reduce power friction.

To learn more: www.projectequinox.net,

Twitter: @Project_Equinox

Facebook: Project Equinox with Andre Paradis

Email: andrecoaching1@gmail.com,

Or call: 213-640-9392

CHAPTER 28

Never Give In. Never Give In. Never, Never, Never Give In!

by James Blakemore

"Never give in. Never give in. Never, never, never, never—in nothing, great or small, large or petty—never give in, except to convictions of honour and good sense. Never yield to force. Never yield to the apparently overwhelming might of the enemy."

This is the exact quote from then-Prime Minister Winston Churchill's famous Never Give In speech given at Harrow School, October 29, 1941 which helped inspire a nation and the world to resist and survive against the threat of one of the worst tyrannies in modern history. The resistance and survival of England against Hitler is truly one of the great stories of our times. However, I had no idea as to how much trouble this philosophy would cause me.

A good friend of mine and fellow author, Greg Reid, once wrote a book titled *Three Feet From Gold*. In that book, he tells the story of a man consumed with gold fever, Mr. Darby. Mr. Darby left home and went west to prospect for gold, which he eventually found. Once he discovered the valuable ore, he returned to his hometown to raise the capital and purchase the necessary equipment to successfully mine the deposit.

When he was properly equipped, he returned to his mine and began digging. What Mr. Darby didn't do, though, was study geology and mining, and obtain all the knowledge necessary to be a successful gold entrepreneur. As he dug into the gold vein and filled his head with visions of riches, the inevitable happened, the gold vein disappeared. He dug further, convinced "his" gold would reappear, but all the work and wishing was for naught. There was nothing but barren rock.

Depressed and dejected, he sold all his tools and equipment to a local junkman for pennies on the dollar and returned home to face all the investors whose money he had lost. End Mr. Darby's story. Enter the junkman, who, by the way, had always dreamed of being in the mining business. The junkman had studied mining, studied rocks and geology, basically done his homework all his life on the subject. When Darby sold him the tools and equipment, he was ready. He went to the mine and evaluated the situation. He knew that gold ran in veins, and deduced where to look. He began working, and using the same equipment Darby sold him for pennies on the dollar plus his own knowledge, dug into a fabulously rich deposit of high-grade ore barely three feet from where Darby stopped digging. Darby literally quit three feet from gold.

Yes, I know this sounds much like the famous story, Acres of Diamond, told countless times by Baptist Minister and Founder of Temple University Russell Conwell. There are probably countless similar stories, however, I lived one in real life.

In the late 1800s, near Salt Lake City, Utah, a US Army officer discovered the Emma Mine, a fabulously rich silver mine, the greatest of the time. Millions of dollars of silver were harvested from this mine, until one day the ore just stopped. As in the previous story, the operators of the mine didn't understand the geology of the area. There were major faults that cut the silver deposit in pieces. The operators had no idea that their silver had been displaced only about one hundred feet. The treasure lay undiscovered for over fifty years until a geologist who studied the area found the continuation of the ore and mined it until, again, it was apparently exhausted. Years later, by virtue of my uncle, a mining engineer and geologist familiar with the mine, and his brother who took a stock position in it to help finance it, I had the opportunity to run that company. I took what was then a virtually worthless company and turned it into a $1.75 million profit.

How did I do this?

The company had been stagnant and considered worthless for many years with no production due to no proven reserves and the low price of silver. My uncle, the geologist and mining engineer, studied the geology of the area and deduced that there was more ore left to be mined.

We set about proving this. We did the exploration, the drilling, sampling, etc., and began to demonstrate the possibility of a new silver discovery.

Now, understand, this mine is in one of the most environmentally sensitive areas of Utah, a canyon used primarily as a recreational area. These are two qualities pretty incompatible with a major mining operation. As you can well imagine, we were under great scrutiny from many people, most of them not too interested in us reopening a major silver mine, bringing with it all the attendant problems, trucks, dust, dirt, pollution, and noise.

Now, sometimes, your most valuable product may not be the most obvious. You might think that my efforts to prove up more silver ore would be directed to opening the mine, operating it, and selling silver—not so. I knew that there was a near impossibility of reopening that mine. The forces that would align against this were so vast and well funded, that even if we could raise the necessary capital, win the countless court battles, and finally get the necessary permits, that would come long after I had passed. The actual value of this company would be to sell it to a buyer who intended to make sure that there was never any mining in that canyon again. That is exactly what I set out to do, and what I ultimately succeeded in doing.

Now, this process took time, money, and energy. LOTS OF TIME! I could easily have quit at any time, and no one would have blamed me. After all, the company had been dormant for nearly 40 years before I made the sale. But, I hung in there, I knew I had something, and just needed to study, learn, take my time, and most of all, NEVER GIVE UP! Ultimately, my persistence paid off when I took an all but abandoned company and turned it into a $1.75 million profit.

My next venture was a different story. I decided to become a real estate developer.

I was going to start small and build a few apartments in a small town that was desperate for housing due to an oil boom. It wasn't long though before I had people filling my head with ideas of going big.

Go big or go home people said. So I went big.

And the problems started.

I sunk over two million dollars of my money into the project over four years. Every time it seemed that I had overcome a problem another popped up. This happened time after time. When one problem was solved, another presented itself.

With Sir Winston's words echoing in my ears, I refused to give up. More time, more money. Another tack, another direction, more money, more problems. More effort, but still no traction.

I had fallen into the Darby trap. I thought I had found my vein of gold, but I hadn't learned the rules, nor had I studied the lay of the land. I thought that I had all I needed, but I didn't realize that some of the people I had hired, people I trusted, had other agendas, agendas that didn't necessarily align with mine. Also, I hadn't counted on hometown politics. Despite my bringing something badly needed to the community, I was still an outsider, and I didn't realize that no matter how much they needed what I wanted to bring, I was not going to get the help I needed from the town to make my project a success. The final blow, the haymaker that sent me to the mat was when the local economic development board voted not to support my project.

My dreams were dashed, dead, and no matter how much persistence I had, no matter how much I refused to quit, no matter how much I gazed at the gruff visage hanging over my desk, there was nothing I could do to resurrect this project.

It passed into the "not good sense" category Churchill referred to.

When did that happen? I couldn't say. Probably long before I realized it. How much useless money was spent? How much time and energy was wasted? I don't know, certainly more than should have been. Much more. Did I learn lessons? Yes, long, expensive, brutal lessons.

But, have I lost my will to persist? Not hardly. I still make mistakes, but I am smarter for them.

My current endeavor? We are constructing housing out of repurposed shipping containers. We take used shipping containers and build houses, offices, and other things from the steel structures.

The idea started when I was still involved with real estate development. I was looking at other towns to develop in, but was told several times that new development wasn't wanted despite a desperate need for workforce housing.

The boom and bust cycles of the oil business would bring new development to a town during the good times, but after the prices declined, as they always did, the workers left, leaving empty houses and apartment complexes to deteriorate and fall apart.

I came up with the idea of an apartment complex built from shipping containers, like so many huge Lego blocks, but before I could implement my idea, the oil business hit a slump, and the housing wasn't needed.

This led to efforts to develop affordable housing and then to housing for Native American tribes. These are both great ideas that are hard to make a reality. Two years I spent courting two different tribes, but with no results. Yes, they needed housing, hundreds of houses. Yes, they wanted us to provide training and jobs desperately needed by their tribal members. But when it came to giving us a firm order and deposit which would justify the time and expense of a manufacturing facility, they just couldn't seem to make it happen. It was one excuse after another.

Have I given up? NOT HARDLY!

Has it paid off big? Not yet, but I am confident it will. I have been working on it about as long as I worked on the development project, but I have not spent the huge sums of money. I've been smarter with what I'm doing and how I'm doing it.

Yes, I've had setbacks. Some projects haven't worked out. People have come and gone. But Churchill's words are still there. If England in its darkest hour can stand alone against Germany's might without surrender, I can persist in business. I have plenty of role models. Edison, Drake, Bell, or more modern examples, Musk, Bezos, Jobs. They all had their setbacks, I can weather mine.

We are currently building workforce housing from shipping containers for the oil boom in west Texas. Have we turned the corner? Not yet, but I see it coming. The corner is in sight.

That mining company I brought back from the brink, I worked with for twenty years before the wonderful moment it put over a million dollars into my pocket. Most of that was part-time, off and on, a week here another there. I was getting to know the history, the players, the personalities. Once I focused my energies on that project and formulated my plan, it was a more modest five years. It was five years of concentrated effort, five years of persistence, five years of not "giving in."

I think it was worth it.

What about you? When was the last time you gave up on your dream? Did you quit just three feet from gold? What about next time? Will you hit the motherlode and write your name across the sky? Best of luck to you and I hope to see you at the top!

TWEETABLE
You never truly fail until you succeed or you truly quit, so never give in, never give in, never, never, never give in!

 *James M. Blakemore is a serial entrepreneur and is currently active in the oil and gas, ranching, real estate, and modular building businesses. He is founder, president, and CEO of Bedford Falls Development and Blakemore Properties of Midland, TX. He is also co-founder and CEO of EverGreen Manufacturing, LLC, manufacturer of unique homes and other structures from repurposed shipping containers. His current project is designing and building modular workforce housing units and communities in the Permian Basin oil fields of west Texas. You can contact him at jblakemore@innovativehabitats.com or visit www.innovativehabitats.com.*

CHAPTER 29

Misery to Marital Bliss

by Ethel Rucker

My marriage started out like many of yours with high aspirations, goals, dreams, and living happily ever after. But to my surprise, the first three years were horrible. We fought continuously: physical altercations, outbursts of anger, adult temper tantrums, the silent treatment, and the list goes on and on. We realized our backgrounds played a significant role in our dysfunctional relationship. I would like to share some the things we discovered that transformed our marriage from pain to pleasure, from pleasure to passion, from passion to purpose, and from "Misery to Marital Bliss."

Let's start with Donald. My husband grew up in a single parent home. He worked in the cotton fields of Mississippi at the age of eight making $35 a day. His father never married his mother. His dad lived in the same city but was not fully engaged in his upbringing. This, of course, left an identity void in Donald's life. He became rebellious and angry. He was angry at everything and everyone. Rejection and self-hatred shaped his outlook and perception on life. My husband developed a belief that women had a place, to be seen but not heard.

My background was similar but with much more violence. My father abandoned our family when I was five years old. My mother decided to move her five children from the South to Pasadena, California. I had neither a father figure or a positive male role model in my childhood. After moving to Pasadena, my mother met and married my stepfather. Having a man in the house brought a sense of security and financial stability. However, sometimes that which we think is a blessing can come packaged with pain. My stepfather had a drinking problem. Our somewhat happy and stable home soon turned into a living nightmare with domestic violence, cursing, physical altercations, gunshots, and constant police visitations. I remember numerous scenes of police officers handcuffing my mother and dragging her down the driveway. This was embarrassing. I also endured constant berating by my mother. Name calling was her weapon of choice for me, such as, "You are the ugliest child I have." Living in this environment, I developed a severe case of low self-esteem, a lack of self-respect, and God knows I had no respect for men.

After being kicked out of the house and experiencing homelessness as a teenager, you can imagine my perspective on marriage and family life was bleak. The one thing that was constant and consistent in my life was church. Church is where I found a sense of purpose, identity, and self-worth. Although, church was a major influence in my life, I still desired to date. As you know, dating brings its own set of troubles and unique challenges. I only mention this because I don't want to paint the picture that I was a saint. Eventually, I realized dating wasn't working for me.

After seeking counsel from the Lord, I decided to take myself out of the dating scene and dedicated myself wholly to church life. No more sex for me outside of marriage! No more going out. No more boyfriends! I became a monk (haha). Truthfully, I totally committed my time, talent, and treasures to a higher purpose. It is here where Donald's and my story begins.

Donald and I met at a church in Altadena. When he walked through the doors of the church, I heard an inward voice speak to me. I didn't hear the angels singing or anything like that! But I heard a soft, peaceful voice telling me 'that's your husband."

Wait, I know what you are thinking, She's crazy! She has lost her mind! However, this is my story, and I'm sticking to it.

I could barely believe it. He was so handsome and fine. Now, remember everything that glitters is not always gold. Donald was truly handsome, but he had some issues. So, I took a leap of faith in response to the soft, peaceful voice. I'm glad I did. More about that later.

I came into my marriage with visions of TV shows like, *I Love Lucy*, *Leave it to Beaver*, and *Ozzie and Harriet*. I know, I'm dating myself. It's amazing how television and reality shows can shape your perspective and set you up for illusions of grandeur. Plus, I was still overcoming rejection, low self-esteem, abandonment issues, and a lack of self-worth. And, Donald had his own internal struggles and feelings. Merging all that, which is what you do in marriage, would require tools and tips we didn't possess. My dream of living happily ever after suffered a major reality check through a nightmare for which I was unprepared.

Our first three years of marriage was full of arguments, physical altercations, weeks of not talking to one another, disagreements, financial woes, and just horrible. It was during this season that I cried out to God. Literally, I cried to God. We needed help and didn't know where to find it. One day, during my quiet time with God, I said Father, because that's really how I see Him, "I know you didn't mean for me to live my life like this. I hated the day that I said I do to this man." As I prayed and sought for answers to turn our marriage around, I heard that soft, peaceful voice again. He said, "I came to give you life and that life more abundantly. You must choose to fight for the marriage you desire." Those words revolutionized our marriage! We began to move from pain to pleasure, from pleasure to passion, from passion to purpose, and from misery to marital bliss.

Every marriage and every relationship needs the right tools and principles for success. We discovered that marriage works just like a business. It requires core principles, vision, rules, and guidelines for success and sustainability. Here are a few of the principles which have propelled our marriage for 35 years into a fruitful, fun-filled, and productive 35-year marriage.

Principle 1: Mutual Submission

When I heard this word, it made my skin crawl. Submit, I don't think so! Submit to a person who I felt didn't deserve my respect. My belief system rejected the word submit. I thought of it as being a doormat with no voice. But after careful study and research, I came to understand the power in submission. Submission is required in every system of regulations. Submission in its basic meaning is strength under control and a system of order which keeps things flowing together. We enjoy the power of electricity because we can house and harness it for our maximum benefits. Submission works the same way in marriage. Each participant in the marriage must be willing to bring the power they possess under a controlled environment. That environment is mutual submission. It's an environment where we mutually submit one to another in reverence to God. Submission doesn't mean you are less but eliminates one party dominating the other and fosters the oneness principle that produces and maintains order in the marriage relationship.

Principle 2: Temperaments

I was led to read a book called *A Spirit Controlled Life* by Tim LaHaye. This book helped us to learn and understand how God wired us. According to my reading, there are four basic temperaments: melancholy, sanguine, choleric, and phlegmatic. Learning our temperaments, or how we're wired from birth, helped to put things in proper perspective. Instead of trying to change one another or fix each other, we begin to celebrate our differences. These differences help balance our marriage relationship. This knowledge birthed in the relationship an appreciation for our strengths and weaknesses. Each person in the marriage brings specific insights, experiences, knowledge, and skills to the marriage. Understanding the others' temperament helps define roles or functionalities in the marriage.

For example, the choleric temperament possesses unique qualities for details, organizing, and leadership. This temperament will function well in the marriage relationship with responsibilities specific to those qualities. They are also often opinionated, self-sufficient, and strong-willed. If paired with a phlegmatic temperament, which possess unique qualities like, being genuinely happy, kindhearted, and sympathetic, the weakness in the choleric can be balanced out by the unique qualities of the phlegmatic.

Principle 3: Rules of Engagement

In every relationship you will have disagreements, intense fellowship, and different perspectives and opinions. Learning to fight fair and have healthy conflict is critical to any successful relationship. Boxing is a perfect metaphor for learning to fight fair in the relationship. In boxing, both fighters are given instructions prior to the fight. Well, likewise, in relationships we need to know the rules of engagement. First, we need to identify each person's style for managing conflict and tension. I outline the four styles that were relevant to our relationship and what we discovered in raising our children in my book. For example, Donald was a stuffer. He was non-expressive and untruthful about how he really felt about situations and circumstances. On the other hand, I was a screamer. I was known to elevate my voice during intense fellowship and disagreements. Of course, my style caused him to shut down and his style cause me to scream. Well, not much was accomplished when he shut down and I was screaming. So, we had to implement rules for engagement. We learned through identifying our style for managing conflict and tension are:

- Eliminate the attitude of being right

- Avoid throwing negative words or accusations or attacking one another

- Be hard on the problem not the person

- No hitting below the belt (statements designed to belittle or berate)

- Realize each person needs something

After discovering the principles mentioned above and more outlined in our book *From Misery to Marital Bliss*, I can truly say I'm extremely blessed with my marriage. Donald and I discovered marriage should be by design and not by default. Many marriages are built on faulty foundations which lead to separation, divorce, and death. The solution to these overwhelming situations is **In Rooted Love**. **In Rooted Love**, is a ministry or product of our pain and many sorrows and it teaches the marriage union is perfect, the people in the marriage are not. Therefore, we have developed principles to assist couples in building and improving their marriage by offering workshops designed to give them the tools and tips needed for a prosperous and purposeful marriage. If we can, you can with the right tools. Merge two visions into a single vision and have a marriage by design instead of marriage by default!

I would like to thank my mentor Kyle Wilson for giving me this amazing opportunity to be a contributor.

TWEETABLE

Marriage is a marathon not a sprint. There is a message in our marital mess and wisdom in our marital bliss. You may have had a bumpy start, but you can have a smooth landing.

Pastor Ethel Rucker co-founded a grassroots ministry Christian Development Center with her husband Pastor Donald Rucker. She spearheads the women's ministry Covenant Daughter of Destiny. She feeds the homeless and needy in her community and teaches marriage enrichment and parenting classes. Her passion is helping marriages and families become whole and healthy. She has over 25 years of experience in education. Ethel has three adult children Daniel, David, and Erikka, a son in love Brandon, and two bonus children Shirley and Anthony. She is an author, speaker, marriage coach, wife, mother, and grandmother.

Inrootedlove@gmail.com | Nrootedlove.com

CHAPTER 30

The Calm During the Storm

by Ben Suttles

I was holding on to a stop sign as the flood water from Hurricane Harvey swept past me. My life flashed before my eyes.

I lost a lot in 2017, even before Hurricane Harvey struck that summer. I broke up with my long-term girlfriend and mother of my daughter, I moved out of my house, and I lost money in bad investment deals. But none of that mattered to me as I clung to that stop sign. I was never going to be able to see my daughter grow up or walk her down the aisle. I would never be able to travel around the world or see the pyramids. This was it.

But then, in my darkest moment, God said, "Let go."

So, I did.

And as the waters took me down the street, and I came ever closer to the now raging creek, I felt the barriers, the fears, and the anxiety that cripples people, that holds them back from achieving greatness, wash away with the flood waters. At that moment, in absence of fear, my head was clear, and I saw my path. I swam to a nearby fence line and held on for dear life as the waders I'd been wearing filled with water and tried to bring me down. But God said, "Not today."

As I dragged myself up the fence line to higher ground, my purpose was clear in my mind. I was going to help not only my parents, my best friend, my daughter, and her mother recover from Hurricane Harvey, but I was also going to start living with a passion to teach people to chase their dreams and not let adversity hold them down. I was going to give back the knowledge I had in business and real estate to give people the opportunity to live up to their fullest potential. My purpose in life was clear. I am here to help.

But it wasn't always like this. When I was in my early 20s I had no idea what I wanted to do. I started off in business with no real skills, no sales training, and no knowledge of how a business was run, but my Dad and Mom showed me how to sell. They showed me how to talk with clients, how to price out products and services, and how to read balance sheets and income statements. It took me awhile, and it was never easy, but I kept at it. I worked hard, and it got easier. I always loved sales, the excitement you get on "the hunt" for new opportunities, and that rush when you're about to close a deal.

But then it started to not be as fun. It started to become routine and not as challenging. So, when my daughter Lillian came along, I was ready to take on a new challenge, fatherhood. This might have been my hardest job to date, and I took it seriously. But I didn't realize going in that she would teach me more about being a better person and how to improve myself than I could have ever imagined. She taught me patience and humility, but ultimately, she gave me the spark that I was losing, the energy I needed to start a new venture.

I will forever be grateful to Lillian and my parents for giving me the skills I needed. Because of them, I had the motivation to go in a totally different direction. I got into real estate. I had read Robert Kiyosaki's *Rich Dad Poor Dad* before Lillian was born, and it was a light bulb moment. It showed me the power and success that could be had from real estate investing if you were hungry enough and motivated enough to go out and make it happen.

I quickly realized I had a full-time, 50-hour a week job, and I wasn't quite sure where to get started. So, like most people who do real estate, I started off in single-family investments. However, after struggling with that, and essentially creating myself another job versus creating a business, I pivoted into multi-family investments (like apartments). I found a mentor and got to work, and like the old saying goes, I had some "beginners luck." I was lucky enough to get my first deal under contract, a 92-unit apartment complex, within four months of taking on this new path, but that luck didn't last, and I was in for a surprise.

I never really had a plan. I never really thought about how I'd turn my "side hustle" into a real business. I also wasn't doing a good job of juggling this venture with my day job. So as time passed between my first deal and my second, I got discouraged.

I thought, *Am I wasting my time doing this? What can I change in the equation to make this more successful and not such a chore?* Then it hit me. I needed to treat this like a true business, set aside time to actually work on it, and just it, and I needed to involve my partners more in keeping up with my pace and plugging in the gaps in my skill set. Lo and behold, we hustled just a tad bit more and got our second deal, a 139-unit apartment complex this time. That one wasn't that easy though and took almost a year to close with us finally going under contract right after Harvey.

The lessons I learned through the years in real estate have taught me valuable lessons that I take with me to this day: be patient, be purposeful, and be passionate about what you're doing. That equals the profit.

The lessons that became so clear after Harvey have catapulted my real estate career in less than a year from two deals to five and from $10MM in assets to $30MM, but I don't look at it as a job. I enjoy the work and I enjoy giving back to people, and I think ultimately that is why I've been successful.

As I look back on Hurricane Harvey, the thousands of homes and businesses that flooded, the people who lost their lives, and the thousands of people still struggling to get on their feet, I thank God that he showed me a better way, a more purposeful way to give back.

The memory of the storm and the rest of the terrible events that year are still fresh, but my purpose in life has been crystallized, and my path in my career is straight as an arrow. I've begun to give back to worthy causes, I've reignited the Meetup event I host here in Houston in order to continue to give back my real estate knowledge, and I've stopped playing things close to the chest. The world doesn't become a better place unless you put yourself out there and make it a better one, so through countless meetings, events, lunches, and dinners, I'm giving back to folks my knowledge on how the world of finance and real estate really works.

I tell my story about Hurricane Harvey as a reminder of two things. First, life is too short to spend it working a job you hate just to pay for stuff you don't need. Second, giving back to folks truly has motivated me to another level, and I want to keep that effort up as the act of giving is truly more rewarding than the act of taking.

I want to inspire people who say, "I can't do real estate with a full-time job," or "I'm too young, inexperienced, broke," whatever it might be, because that's simply not true. We're all capable of incredible things. Sometimes those things are hard to figure out, but then sometimes things happen in our life that jar us from our daily routine and show us what we're truly capable of. Keep your eyes open for them, strive to find them, pursue them, and one day you'll find your purpose too.

TWEETABLE

The act of giving is more rewarding than the act of taking. Don't play things close to the chest, share your knowledge, share your successes, and give back, because one day you might inspire someone to do something great. The world needs more givers.

Ben Suttles lives and works in Houston and hopes to inspire people that regardless of how tough life is or how many barriers you think you have stacked up against you, you can go out and create a better life for yourself and your family through hard work, dedication, and pursuit of knowledge. He owns over half a dozen companies with revenues of over $8 million, and currently manages $30 million in real estate assets while helping raise his four-year-old daughter. You can reach him direct at ben@disruptequity.com or through disruptequity.com.

CHAPTER 31

What Wasn't Supposed to Be Became More Than a Miracle

by Mahealani Trepinski

I am so thankful that I am here. I am truly on this Earth for a purpose! My mother was not supposed to get pregnant with me, as she was on an IUD birth control device. Then she went into labor three and a half months early. The doctors told my mother and father that I may not make it to see the light of day. I was born around midnight and was only 3 lbs 2 oz. Then I dropped to 2 lbs. 3 oz. My father could hold me in the palm of his hand.

After surviving my premature birth and month and a half in the neonatal intensive care unit (NICU), my challenges continued. I had to grow up with a verbally abusive father, and one of my brothers sexually abused me which I suppressed until my first marriage. This led to many issues at home, personally, and at school. I tried to end my life three times during junior high and high school because I couldn't handle the things that were going on around me. When I was a senior, it should have happened with the pills that I took. I truly feel that God pulled me through this and helped me survive. I do not know any other reason why I survived this attempt.

Upon graduating high school, I thought that I would want to help others like me and be a child counselor. However, with dyslexia, school was a huge challenge. At that time, education environments were just starting to understand what dyslexia was. Plus I was not sure if I would be able to separate myself from each client and not get emotionally involved. In light of this huge unassisted challenge, I felt that I should pursue other avenues for my future. I started thinking I would want to do something that still involved helping people and kids, and I looked at becoming an athletic trainer because it is more hands-on and would be easier for me to do.

As I was about to head off to Tarleton State University, my (now) ex-husband came into my life which caused me to focus on other things rather than pursuing my career as an athletic trainer. I was married at 21, and the marriage lasted until I was 23. This marriage was abusive in every aspect you can imagine. The marriage finally came to an end when he had an affair. I thank God I was able to get out of that horrible situation.

After I was divorced and had moved back home, I did all kinds of jobs to support my 15-month-old son. If I continued to pursue a job as an athletic trainer at a high school, I would never be there for my son; I would always be at school. Before and after school and on holidays for sporting events, I would have needed to work. So, as a single mom, I decided it would not be in my son's best interest. I knew that I wanted to do something in the healing field. I had wanted to be an athletic trainer to help impact our kids today as my coach did for me when I was in school.

I still wanted to do that for people, but I went and worked for corporate America where I met my best friend and father-figure to my son. Later, after we both left corporate America, he became the love of my life and husband. I left corporate America because I did not like that I felt limited, and I went and worked for a few different chiropractors to see if I wanted to do that. There, I kept feeling that God was telling me to go to massage school. I thought, "Massage is not healing people. It is just fluff."

Was I wrong. I went to school and saw that there was a medical aspect to massage. I started out as a massage therapist and still serve in that capacity today. I have been in the natural healing field for over 15 years. I am a well-tuned intuitive specialist in craniosacral, energy work, medical massage, and other services. I have also been a practicing health and life coach since 2012. I started speaking and leading spiritual retreats in 2008 part-time. A few ladies from church and I started a non-profit ladies retreat for women of all denominations where I led them in praise and worship. Eventually, it evolved into a couples retreat, and after four great years, we allowed it to dissolve.

I feel that I am supposed to help those in need heal their mind, body, and soul. My passion is healing people by education and helping to bring the mind, body, and soul to homeostasis. I feel that a naturally healthy, clean body will lead to living a very long life without a lot of the issues bodies normally have in the aging process. I believe that putting the mind, body, and soul in a natural, healthy state will bring the body harmony and not allow negativity to emerge. For example, by healing the body naturally through food, proper body treatments, and healing the mind, you will not have to take drugs that will cause negative things in the body. The result is living a long, healthy life. It is never too late to reverse the negative issues that have already started. The sooner you start taking care of yourself, the longer you will live without issues.

Doing your passion and what you love to do can also bring money in. In the past, this was not always the case because I would not always value myself monetarily. I wanted to help people for little or no cost. I kept saying that God would take care of me because I was doing work that He put me in. Although this turned out to be true (He did pull me through, and at times I did not know how He was going to do so.), you can serve while charging what your services are worth.

So, I hired a business coach and a bookkeeper to help me run my business as a business. I even opened a natural healing center and spa and including a full staff of medical massage therapists, natural estheticians, a Christian hypnotherapist counselor, a natural chiropractor, and a medical-grade far infrared sauna. I was the health and life coach.

Then God gave me another turn. Not one, but two, surprise babies. My husband and I tried for a couple of years to have babies, but I kept having miscarriages. After the third miscarriage, we decided to remodel the house, and I opened the natural healing center and spa that I just mentioned and also went back to school for integrative nutrition. Around six months later I was pregnant, and then the first baby girl was born.

I was in labor for over 26 hours. When my daughter was born, she was Apgar one. She had a spinal tap her first day of life and was hooked up to all kinds of machines to keep her living. She was in the NICU for five days, and I also had a lot of things not right with me. I was in the hospital for five days getting my counts back to homeostasis. My specialist doctor told me that it would be a miracle if I were to get pregnant again because of all the trauma my body went through with the baby girl. So, after the healing, I went back to work with my sweet pea.

Six months later, my staff kept saying, "We think you are pregnant again."

And I said, "No, it can't be. My body is just going back to normal."

One day they brought in a test and made me take it. Lo and behold, I was pregnant! I went to the doctor and found out that I was three months pregnant with a baby when the doctors swore it would be a miracle if I were to become pregnant again. During the birth I had a placental abruption and surprise baby number two was actually born dead. She drowned in my blood from the abruption. Fortunately, the NICU medical staff was able to bring her back to life. The doctor's first words to me were, "If I were thirty seconds later, your daughter would not be here. If I were a minute to two minutes later, you and I would not be having this conversation." The doctors stated that she could have brain issues. Thank you to God she is wonderfully healthy baby girl. She is doing awesome with no issues. So, as you see, I am supposed to be here for a reason and God has a purpose for me!

When God gave me two surprise babies, I decided to close the healing center prematurely so that I could be a spend more time being a mom. I would go back to doing part-time work. My life was all over the place. My husband and I decided that I would start working with a contract sales company that worked well with my integrative nutrition. I loved it and was making awesome money with it, but it was a "job." My passion business was suffering for it. So, I started focusing on my passion again, and guess what, it started to flourish once more. I truly believe when you do what you were meant to do and love doing it, it shows, and the money comes in too. I do have to say, the paychecks of the heart (paychecks that are not monetary but true, heartfelt gifts that mean something to you) are there as well. It is great to see something I love to do thrive!

I love aiding people in this journey. It does not seem like work to me. I enjoy every minute of helping people heal. It makes my heart happy to be in a career that makes me feel this way. I am so blessed to be doing what I am doing and thankful that God brought me to this. I have noticed when I let go and let God, my work (his work) falls into place. He brings the clients, patients, and business opportunities to me. Then everything starts to really go and flourish! I love life! I love to help heal others and love to educate people as well! I do hope that you can have the same joy I have. No matter what you have gone through in the past, the past is not what is ahead of you. I want to be a winner, not a victim! I want to stand and raise my experiences from my past to use them to not only make me stronger but also to help others become stronger.

I hope that you too can say that you love what you do and that things are falling into place for you. I pray and wish the best for you. I hope you are inspired to go be the best you can be and to love what you do! You can do anything, even if you have had bad things happen to you in the past or circumstances that say otherwise. That is the past, so let it go and only look forward to your bright, shining future that you are meant to have! Because in reality, life is just too short! Ask God for his help daily and strive to do his will. Put forth the work that needs to be there and He will have everything fall into place as it should be.

TWEETABLE

No matter what happens to you in life, choose to be the better you that you can be.

Mahealani Trepinski will help you go deeper to achieve your dreams and newfound health. Mahealani is a speaker and life and health coach as well as a well-tuned intuitive specialist in craniosacral, medical massage therapy and integrative nutrition.

She speaks on many topics from natural health, to reaching your goals, to inspiration. If you would like to have Mahealani speak at your next engagement, email Mahealani@healingmasters.us. For a free Skype consult, visit ahawaiiantouch.com.

CHAPTER 32

Fear and Self-Doubt are the Greatest Killers of Personal Success

by Dana Samuelson

I am a professional numismatist. Most of you probably need to look that up, but I'll make it easier for you. I am a nationally recognized US rare coin dealer specializing in pre-1933 US gold coins. I'm also one of the luckiest guys on the planet. I love what I do, and I do what I love. But there was a time when I thought I was the unluckiest guy on the planet, and it was exactly that streak of trouble that freed me. I took one of the worst things that could ever happen to anyone and turned that into one of the best things that ever happened to me.

Having been raised in the 60s and 70s, I was lucky to see how both conservatives and liberals lived. I was raised in a conservative family and was taught to be obedient: go to school, get a job, join the establishment, and be a productive member of society. At the same time, it was impossible not to see the culture that the 60s created of love your brother, be free, and be wary of the establishment.

While my parents were teaching me values from the 1940s and 1950s, coming of age in the 60s and 70s informed my personal experience. Young men my brother's age, just five years older than me, were being sent off to Vietnam and coming home in caskets.

Life was exciting, society was changing fast, and it was confusing. My older brother Clark guided me through the maze of contradictions and confusion. He was not just my older brother, he became my mentor, and he took me under his wing. He talked to me, explained things, and helped me see and understand both sides of what was happening.

When I graduated college in 1980, with a German degree of all things, completely unhireable because the economy was in the tank and interest rates and inflation were over 15%, Clark helped me get my first job in the precious metals and rare coin business. As someone already in the business, he vouched for me as honest and trustworthy, imperatives in our business. That's how I got my first job in the industry that I love, one that I will continue to participate in, one way or another, probably until I die. Old coin dealers never seem to retire, they just seem to slow down a bit.

My career was a study of advancement. Over the next 18 years, I learned everything I needed to learn to go into business for myself. My career path was the equivalent of starting out as the dishwasher and working up to owning the restaurant. I was lucky. I made connections with the biggest dealers in the country through the various jobs I held. I traveled all over the United States to coin shows, and I got to spend a lot of my boss's money buying and selling coins and precious metals.

I started in the vault of a large operation counting, weighing, and shipping enormous amounts of physical gold and silver. I did have the opportunity to hold the 1804 Dexter Beresford specimen silver dollar that my boss bought at the ANA summer auction in 1982 for $250,000. That coin traded for almost $3 million recently; it's a beautiful coin, one of 14 known. I got to handle that coin in my hand! But this was the exception to an otherwise dead end, bottom of the totem pole position, but I learned a lot and worked hard.

When on a visit, the buyer from Blanchard & Co., Joe Buzanowski, noticed my strong work ethic and offered me a way out. I was taught how to grade and appraise historical US coins. In my nine years at Blanchard & Co., the largest mail order coin company in the US in the 1980s, I eventually became a mentee of Jim Blanchard (James U Blanchard III, the person most responsible for the private regulation of gold ownership in 1974 in the US). I helped Jim with his personal precious metals and rare coin portfolio and handled some of the most incredible pieces of our country's heritage, rare US gold and silver coins from the 1800s and 1900s. It was incredibly rewarding.

In 1988, Jim sold the company, and many of us moved on. I continued learning, and I made a few more stops along the way, and at this point, I had more practical experience than most others in the industry. I had worked in every area of the coin business from the ground up. I had all the ingredients I needed to start my own company.

But when it came time for me to quit being an employee and become my own boss, I couldn't pull the trigger. I was unhappy with where I was working and who I was working for, but deep down I was scared. I had a wife and a mortgage and taking the leap of faith to start my own business was too intimidating a line for me to cross.

And then one day in 1998, Clark headed off to a coin show in California and was killed in a car accident. Suddenly and out of nowhere, the person who had been most influential in my life, whose career I had followed, and who taught me the most of anyone, was gone.

Up to this point in time I had lived an idyllic life. The sun always shown. The bills were always paid, there were always things to do, wonderful places to vacation at, concerts to go see, new restaurants to try. And now, all that changed in the blink of an eye.

Filled with grief, shock, and sadness, I sat back, looked at myself in the mirror, and said to myself, what are you afraid of? You've just lost one of the most important things you'll ever have in your life. What more can you lose that's worse than that? And the answer I came up with was: nothing. I quickly quit my job and I started my own business.

I didn't realize it at the time, but American Gold Exchange was born out of the grief I was channeling. I took all that furious energy and started a mail order business of my own with it. In the summer of 1998, we were all worried about the computer clocks going bad at the stroke of midnight in 2000. I began selling Y2K Hard Money Survival Packs through a survivalist newsletter. They contained proportionate amounts of "spendable" trading-sized gold and silver coins, and I sold a ton of them. It was so crazy. I stepped into an opportunity and made a ton of money, all the while completely blind with grief.

Y2K came and went, and nothing happened. But, I had sold a lot of bulk metal to people at the bottom of the market. In 1998 and 1999 those financial insurance packs traded for about $3,500 each and were meant to be used for trading coins in case of a breakdown in the system. By 2011, when a different crisis arrived, those hard money packs were worth over $17K each. Even today, those hard money packs are still worth over four times what my customers paid for them in 1998 and 1999.

So, over the long haul, gold and silver are a valuable hedge against currency debasement, especially in an environment like now, when they're printing so much money and wealth is so far off the scale relative to what it's been for generations.

Without a principled financial system, like the one man had for over 2000 years, backed by gold or silver, another and a larger global fiscal crisis is inevitable. When today's piles of paper money start to burn, it's all going to burn at the same time, and it's going to be bad. When push comes to shove, real money will hold its value, and real money is gold and silver.

My company has succeeded because we use our substantial experience and expertise to make sure our clients get what is best for them. What's best for our client is best for us. That has always been my bottom line. And we always say what we do and do what we say.

Today, I enjoy owning a very successful and yet challenging business with tens of thousands of satisfied clients across the country. I've also been voted by my peers President of the Professional Numismatists Guild, the leading organization of rare coin dealers in the US. Being the head of my business has allowed me to spend quality time with amazing people who I never would have met like Jim Rogers, Doug Casey, Robert Kiyosaki, Robert Helms, and authors of *Prosper!* Chris Martenson and Adam Taggart. I have the opportunity to travel the US extensively, going to coin shows and seeing the world. The coin business is full of brilliant misfits, and I am glad to call them my family.

Clark's death broke me, and his loss drastically changed my perception of life and how I viewed living it. Sadly, and happily, that helped me to change my path and start my company. I would have never done it if something like that hadn't happened. I was too scared I would fail and my own fear got in my way. I had been trained to go into the system, get a good job, provide, have security, get the house, get the mortgage...all those things. I did that, but I found that I wanted more, and I could do more. I am so grateful because, even considering this great loss, I've never been happier in my entire life. Fear and self-doubt are the greatest killers of personal success. What have you got to lose? You have one life. You may as well take a chance.

TWEETABLE

Take a chance. Push through fear to go after your dreams. What do you truly have to lose?

Dana Samuelson, professional numismatist, is a nationally recognized US rare coin dealer specializing in pre-1933 US gold coins. With more experience and technical knowledge than almost anyone in the field, Dana helps individuals balance their portfolios with gold and silver and serves rare coin collectors. For his advice on building real, generational wealth, contact Dana at American Gold Exchange.

800-613-9323

dana@amergold.com

www.amergold.com

CHAPTER 33

Paving the Road to a Billion Dollars in Your 20s

by Alex Monéton

"The best way to become a billionaire is to help a billion people."
– Peter H. Diamandis

My grandfather was a tough man. He was a dreamer. As my father would say, he saw school mostly from the outside, preferably on the other side of the fence. He was an entrepreneur at heart and found his path early on. He built his career in the onset of the golden years that followed World War II in Europe. At 21, he did an apprenticeship with a local grocer, but like so many entrepreneurs I've gotten to know over the years, his disdain for authority quickly led to him having to look for work elsewhere. True to himself and his vision, he borrowed $5,000 from his father-in-law to start his own grocery store. 30 years later, he had built a multi-million dollar international clothing empire.

Upon retirement, discovering the power of leverage and time, he would go on to invest his personal wealth diligently, compounding it exponentially over the next 38 years. He believed that the world population would get older, sicker, and more obese as the years went on and invested accordingly. At the age of 88, he passed away, wealthier than he could have dreamed of.

Throughout my life, my grandfather's philosophy and perspectives would be intrinsically linked to mine and my identity as a man.

In the fall of 2012, I moved to Copenhagen to be closer to my then-girlfriend who was studying there. By coincidence, she had picked the city where my grandfather and grandmother lived. Having lived abroad for more than ten years, I welcomed the opportunity to be close to them again. Every Sunday, I would take the train up to their house and we would have lunch. These weekly meetings profoundly deepened our connection.

My grandparents had two chairs facing each other specifically for the purpose of having one-on-one conversations with family and friends. Sitting in the two chairs, my grandfather and I would talk. We would talk a bit about school. Then we'd talk about family—how everyone was doing and the latest news from the ones I didn't keep in touch with. And then, finally, when we were both ready, we'd talk business. More specifically, we would discuss investments. He'd tell me about his perspectives, his theories, and outlooks, what he was buying, what he was selling, and most importantly, why.

To this day, I hold his investment theses and philosophies close to my heart.

◆

I made my first real estate purchase in the summer of 2015. I was 24 years old and living in my home country: France. But my risk-on instinct told me to look elsewhere. So I bought a 1,000 square foot apartment in the Beverly Hills of Colombia, Medellin's El Poblado area. A few months later, I bought a second one. Having lived in 10 different countries throughout my life, I had developed a taste for traveling, and my investment philosophy became ever the more international because of it. Living in places like China and Papua New Guinea showed me that in the most unexpected places opportunities are plentiful. By looking outward, to the world, I could go chase the great deals where others wouldn't dare. Here was a country on the verge of coming out of the longest civil war in modern history. I had what seemed to be an informational advantage over the world that still viewed Colombia as a haven for drug criminals. And I had a key advantage over institutional investors that all private investors share and should leverage: the ability to invest anywhere and in anything.

Over the years, I would discover three more critical advantages private investors have over institutional managers, which made me more money than I can think of: the ability to be concentrated, much longer time horizons, and the lack of career risk. No one is going to fire you for making mistakes when you invest on your own account. You can, therefore, take the risks you need to take.

For the few years following my investments in Colombia, I was living the dream. I was making six figures per year taking advantage of opportunities nobody else saw. I invested in art, obscure emerging markets, and foreign currencies, among other opportunities, and was traveling the world. I spent weekends with my friends all across Europe and could work from anywhere. I was investing, and I was doing well.

In 2016, I traveled to Rio de Janeiro with some friends, only to meet the woman who would become the love of my life. We were attending a street party in a lively barrio, and there she was. Her eyes crossed mine, and I instantly fell in love with her. One day when our kids grow up, they will read this story. And hopefully, they will smile as much as I am right now.

For much of the next year, we traveled the world—and I kept investing. We lived in Morocco, Mexico, Canada, and Spain. She started asking me about the impact of my investments, planting the seed of a greater duty. She was shocked I could be investing in oil given its impact on the planet. She would constantly challenge my investments and my lifestyle because of the impact it had on future generations. She asked me about a greater vision for what I was doing, but I had none.

In the fall of 2017, I officially went into depression. We had moved back to Canada and were living at my girlfriends' parents' house while we found our own place. I was making money and had just sold out of my most lucrative trade ever—in three months I had made $250,000.

But I was miserable. I had the feeling I was throwing my life away. I had big dreams but saw no way of making them happen. I felt as if I had gone too long on the wrong path.

I was dying to do something bigger with my life. The seed that had been planted in my head had grown, but I couldn't get myself to do anything about it. I just loved making money too much to care. Later, I would come to see a lack of alignment between one's personal values and actions as one of the main drivers of discontent in modern society and a common theme among people who become even mildly successful financially.

In short, I had isolated myself from the world.

A few months later, I attended an investment conference in the Caribbean, held on a cruise. I needed to do something about my situation. I had so many questions.

Robert Kiyosaki, author of **Rich Dad Poor Dad**, the bestselling personal finance book of all time, walked on stage talking about big things: big projects, big numbers, big impact. Here was the man who got me into investing 10 years prior, talking about reaching millions through his educational tools to help empower people to make better decisions. His mission is to elevate the financial well-being of humanity. That is no sissy goal. It was powerful, and partly because I was desperate, I listened carefully.

The year prior I had started investing in blockchain assets and protocols. I had a strong interest in the revolutionary technology these systems could bring to the world. I could imagine potential for a huge impact. I didn't know how to scale impact investments yet, but I would soon find out.

That same night, I went to play basketball on the deck. That is when I met John.

John had been a major in the Air Force, recently retired. John seemed like an exemplary father and an honest man. Glen was there too, a successful business owner in his 50s, along with two of my millennial roommates on the ship. In between a game, Glen sat us down and asked each of us:

> "You guys are young. You have your whole life ahead of you. Everything that you are learning now, I wish I could have learned at your age. So tell me, what do you want to accomplish, and most importantly, why?"

We thought about it for a bit. We then took turns to explain how we wanted to invest to make money and create more freedom for ourselves. Although I had no answer that I remember being convincing, my heart told me to think bigger. I needed to do something impactful with my life. I needed to step up. I knew it, and there was no way around it. And then John spoke.

> *"I do it for the legacy I want to leave behind. I realize this is all much bigger than me, and that everything is interconnected. Only by doing good will I do well for myself. I want to leave a legacy of value behind by impacting the lives of millions of people with the work that I do.*
>
> *I want to provide a service that is genuinely value-adding to people who desperately need it. And I know that if I strive to provide first, and give, then I will receive. It's all about the legacy. It's all about helping people."*

As if someone had orchestrated the cruise to nail the message into my brain, his words hit me hard, and they hit me right when I needed to hear them. It was like everything that had been aching inside of me for two years had finally come to surface. It was a wave of clarity, and I needed to face it, right now, on the spot.

Inside my head I made a life-altering decision. I had been searching for an answer, and now I had found it. I thought back to what Robert Kiyosaki had said. I thought back to making an impact. I thought back to my grandfather. What kind of legacy was I leaving? I didn't know exactly what John did, but I knew that if he had worked it out, I could too.

It was like lightning had hit me. And I wanted to cry.

The idea of making an impact had been inside of me for a long time. Before this time my idea of helping others had been raising or donating funds to charities, supporting those in need and starting a scholarship at my alma mater to support entrepreneurial students in need. But this was different. This was much bigger. This was a lifelong commitment to doing good at a large scale.

Upon returning from the cruise, I promised myself to never engage professionally and personally with anything that wasn't entirely aligned with my personal values and my desire to have a positive impact on the world.

When I found out that John was building homes for seniors, I knew I had found my passion project.

The close relationship I enjoyed with my grandparents throughout the later part of their lives had planted the seed of a special fondness for the elderly. I realized that retirees in their older years form a marginalized part of society, and giving them the chance to have a home and care surrounded by others in the same situation would help them overcome loneliness. I realized that our conversations and lunches were an opportunity not just to lay the foundation for my career as an investor but also a deep desire to provide companionship for an elderly couple whose needs were nothing more than to talk, share, and feel loved. My time giving them this and learning from them were some of the most rewarding memories I have had as an adult.

Today, I am on the path to owning my first several assisted living homes for seniors—the first several of hopefully hundreds.

I actively invest in private companies and technologies that are eager to positively contribute to the world. I am fascinated with blockchain technology, which I believe to be one of the most powerful opportunities to build wealth with impact since the birth of the Internet.

I am also organizing the first of hopefully many conferences called Building Wealth With Purpose to help millennials see past the financial rewards they seek and into making a greater impact for the benefit of all. I've stopped dreaming small and stopped focusing on the money. I have gone back to the days of dreaming big, dreaming of the impact I could have on millions, if not billions of people around the world. And this thought is what gives me fire in the morning.

Ask yourself, what legacy do you want to leave behind? What do you want to be remembered for, and what kind of impact do you want to have on the world? I believe every person is born good with love for others and a heart that is destined to care for the well-being of society. Commit to being purposeful, acting in alignment with your personal values, and for the benefit of others. You will achieve levels of wealth and fulfillment you could only have dreamed of before.

TWEETABLE

Commit to being purposeful, acting in alignment with your personal values, and for the benefit of others. You will achieve levels of wealth and fulfillment you could only have dreamed of before.

Alex Monéton is a private investor with extensive entrepreneurial and investment experience across developed and emerging markets. He actively develops and invests in impact-driven businesses. He is French and Danish and currently resides in Canada. To get in touch with him email at alex@moneton.no.

CHAPTER 34

Doing It "Right"

by Takara Sights

There have been times when I thought I had everything figured out. I would learn something new about life, and as a result, things for me would feel like they were going pretty well. I would think I had gotten to the true core of life, the universe, and everything, and I would shudder to think of how ignorant I was before I had this new realization.

Off the top of my head, I think I had this wise and accomplished feeling when I won Robert Kiyosaki's game Cashflow for the first time, when I had my first kiss, after I read Dale Carnegie's *How to Win Friends and Influence People*, when I declared my major in college, when I moved into my first apartment, and many times when I heard a golden nugget at events like Kyle Wilson's inner circle masterminds.

Each time this happened, I thought it was the last time. One epiphany and I thought I was on top of the world. I thought I would ride this wave of truth and higher consciousness to the end of my life, finally having become the wise soul I crave to be.

How ludicrous! It was only a matter of time before another challenge presented itself, and I realized I did NOT have it all figured out. Despite how obvious it sounds now, it took me years, 26 years, to figure out that I will never reach this point I imagined I was reaching, that I was actively seeking, of having it "all figured out." The universe is just too big, too complex, too awesome for one little me to consider in every moment throughout the day as I make the decisions that create my life.

Surprisingly, when I realized that I would never reach this place (or really, when I was told by the Mark Manson in his popular book *The Subtle Art of Not Giving a F****), I experienced a wave of relief. Once I let go of the expectation that I would understand everything, (which was difficult to do as I pride myself on being a lifelong learner, striving to know as much as I can), I realized that nobody expected me to have it all figured out. Nobody else has it all figured out either! Even though sometimes, especially on social media, it sure seems like it.

There are so many books, people, and ideologies in our current time that tell us that we need to discover and fulfill our one true purpose. There is an idea that there is something each of us is supposed to do. I used to believe this. The other Millennials I talk to often seem to feel this way as well. The idea that there is a path set out for me and that my life is worthless if I do not walk upon that path became a source of regular anxiety as I sought to design a life for myself after I moved out of my mom's house and into my first apartment and a new stage of adulthood in Los Angeles. For the first time, I felt the full weight of how my decisions would impact the rest of my life. It was terrifying.

I was desperate not to mess up. I was desperate not to make the wrong choice by choosing the wrong apartment, the wrong romantic partner, the wrong volunteer opportunity, the wrong month to spend a little extra on eating out, the wrong friends. Any day I could say, not say, wear, not wear, miss, not miss, eat, not eat the wrong thing and ruin my life because it wasn't the "right" way, the planned way.

I'm putting it dramatically, but there were times when my chest could about burst from the pressure of this fear, especially when it came to what I felt were the big decisions. I was waiting to hear what so many call the voice of God, telling me which way to go so that I wouldn't mess up and become a failure.

When making a decision, I had feelings and opinions regarding my options, and I can say I even had a voice in my mind. But I couldn't figure out if the voice was some higher power or fear. The struggle of discerning this caused me a lot of anxiety as I tried to live my life. I asked around for advice from people who seemed in touch with the subject, I started going to a love-centered, accepting church, and I started meditating.

These practices helped. Letting go of my desire to control the future and to figure out what is best before I ever make a mistake was painful, but I am releasing. As our snow queen Elsa said, "Let it go." Over time, listening to my new mentors, I realized that I make my own destiny. Nobody has it figured out, so I can choose to see the world in the way that best suits me. That gives me peace.

And this is how I see it for me right now. I don't have to find one purpose and walk one path. There is no path from which I can stray. There is life. And I create my life through a series of my choices. My choices are my own to make. I have desires and passions. I can turn those desires and passions into goals I want to achieve. Those goals are up to me to choose, and I can go after outcomes I want. How great! I only get to find out how my choices will unfold when they do.

The final piece for me came from Kim Kiyosaki when she spoke only to the Millennials on The Real Estate Guys Investor Summit at Sea. If you are pursuing a goal, if you are moving, you are making ripples in the world. Your actions have consequences, and those consequences, the way you affect others around you, intended or unintended, are your purpose. You may never know what your purpose is, but if you are making decisions and you are moving, you are fulfilling it.

We live in a society designed to exacerbate anxiety. But our purpose is one thing we can stop being anxious about. Do things you enjoy that benefit others. Serve others. Help others. If you do so, in the present you will know you are doing good in the world. Enjoy yourself. Make an adventure of it. What do you like to do? How can you benefit others by doing it? That's all you need. Try a dodgeball league. Volunteer at the zoo. Attend that knitting Meetup. Take yourself to dinner alone. Fly to Turkey. Let's play! As you go, have faith that your true purpose is taking care of itself.

TWEETABLE

Your purpose is to pursue your passion and in doing so to benefit others. Let go of the pressure to get it right.

Takara Sights is an editor, book lover, and Amazon #1 bestselling author. Forever the playful adventurer, she now lives in Los Angeles creating spaces for LGBT people of color to celebrate their successes and unique journeys. For more like this, subscribe at takarasights.com. Connect!

Instagram: @takarasights

Snapchat: takeezi

CHAPTER 35

An Empire Builder's Path to Purpose

by Troy Hoffman

No greater gift could be opened than the ever-long journey of discovering your soul's purpose.

People want the quick fix, the now, the dopamine of the truth of who they are and who they ever will be. We long for it. We search for it. When we don't find it, we numb the shit out of ourselves and find ways to hide. We sedate ourselves through alcohol, food, sugar, Netflix, porn, meaningless sex, drugs, and an endless cycle of self-help books, tapes, and seminars. We are disconnected and yet trying to find true connection to Source, whatever that is.

And in the end, when we attempt to follow the examples of others are we closer to finding the joy of truly knowing who we are? Or are we more confused by the examples of others than the truest discovery of self? The truest discovery of self is accomplished through the pain and self-reflection of subjective experiences that end up defining the truth of what we are capable of. Our self is not what we might be able to realize in actuality in the future, because the future never truly manifests. The ONLY person we are is who we are at this moment. We are the one we have chosen to take daily action to become, based on what direction we are pursuing in single moments in time.

WHY? Why do I say this? This is me. This was me. This is my journey. My path. The continual march through this life pursuing this inner voice that constantly calls me to be more. Do more. Impact more. Discover more.

1. F*$% what others think, starting now. This is stage one to truly knowing you.

This is the first lesson I had to learn. Others' intent, however well intentioned, of where my life should go or who I should become, will not define my destiny. I had a college professor say I was a terrible speaker who couldn't follow a stupid three-point outline. #StillCan't. If I had followed other's intentions for me, I would not have spoken in front of over 100,000 people at this point in my life!

2. Stop lying. This is stage two. After you don't care, you can actually start telling the truth.

I lie to myself all the time. I lie about where I actually am. I often paint the picture of my reality as too great or too dismal. I often omit the facts or imagine a more glamorized version of them. I downplay what I have done sometimes or play it up too much. I lie about my real effort and the time I spent in an area. I start thinking I'm getting results from my actions despite long, hard looks at the facts. I may say I'm loving when what I am doing may not be a true loving action for them as it is for me.

3. Ask yourself, do I even care about finding the real me? This is stage three.

If you dare to open Pandora's box and begin the pain, suffering, and life-altering process you will continue to undergo, then you are ready. You will seek, you will find, you will knock, and the door will be opened.

I was 17 and an ocean rescue professional lifeguard. Being paid $6.75 an hour, I was on top of the world. I didn't even know that so much more than beaches, babes, and bars lay ahead of me. That is, until someone invited me to an Amway seminar. He talked of traveling down the Rhine in a river boat with his family and flying all over the US to hang at their vacation houses. He was also impacting lives of those who were depressed and felt they couldn't live on. See, the day I first heard how large a dream could be was only six months after a guy who got kicked out of his house came to live with me and committed suicide. I CARED. I knew that I would not let this happen around me again.

4. Practice strategic self-reflection until you really discover YOU. This is stage four. If you are still reading, then you actually have a shot of discovering your true soul's purpose.

At 17, I knew that whatever money I made was going to buy books and tickets to seminars. It was apply or die! I dove into self-help wholeheartedly for the next 25 years. I sit here now today and have done more, seen more, and built more than I ever dreamed possible.

Knowing this, will you do what is required? Will you subject yourself to reading and taking massive action until you succeed or fail? For God's sake, stop talking about what you are going to do and instead DO something until it gets some kind of real result. Good or bad, I don't care! Just go! Go!

Ok. Now, you can actually look at the facts of action taken and say what worked and what didn't, and ask yourself, *What must I discover about myself next?*

See, it is life-long, daily discovery through years of repeated analysis and clear documentation of the thoughts, feelings, and results along this path.

If you pick up *Think and Grow Rich* and apply the lessons within, you will find the scars will be many and deep. And each scar is a reminder of what to do and not to do to achieve what that voice inside your head whispers so fragilely to you. If you do not listen, if you do not risk, if you do not leap, you will never know.

5. Employ the scientific process of discovery. This is stage five. Think Jackson Five!

Fame and fortune await with this last detailed analysis after you have some real deep perspective to guide you.

WORDS. They frame us and define us. Create personal clarity with the definition and meaning you give to them. What are the words you will choose to define your soul's mission statement?

My mission statement so far is, "I am an empire builder and legacy leaver. I help people find, follow, and finish their course of destiny."

It may change. But the ever-evolving journey has landed me here.

I also highly recommend an analysis of your gifts and strengths.

The five I recommend in a work-life context are:

1. Kolbe Index
2. Color Code
3. Astrowow
4. DISC
5. Harrison Assessments

The goal of each report is to simply read. Then, circle the top 10 things that jump out to you and ring clear with that inner voice. Then, analyze and see which things across the reports and across the years of data ring true. Part of the value of this is that you paid a price to get this information, which gets you on massive action.

I did these reports over and over, year after year to see how I changed and what continually rang true for decades. I am a servant leader. I am a quick start. I am loyal. I am all over the place with daily disciplined action and structure. I am not detail-oriented. Too many tasks and I'm swimming in a sea of chaos. Still, I move things massively forward. I care for people and impact lives. I give. I love. I cherish people. I like building things that impact people and I like being a part of something greater than myself.

At the end of this, we discover our purpose which impacts people. And, if done right, our purpose will bring endless profits of love, joy, fulfillment, health, and financial abundance. I hold this truth to be self-evident.

The only thing I'll ever ask of you is this. You've got to promise not to stop, even when you feel there is no way you can go on.

 ## TWEETABLE
If done right, our purpose will bring endless profits of love, joy, fulfillment, health, and financial abundance.

TROY HOFFMAN – EMPIRE BUILDER AND LEGACY LEAVER

SIMPLURIS- Founder – 3 Time INC 500 List – FSU100 Honoree

If you want help on this journey, my cell is 850-322-8261.

Website: troyhoffman.com

CHAPTER 36

When Your Purpose Is Bigger Than Your Pain

3 Keys to Success

by Jennifer Thompson

I grew up in the small farm town of Eula, Texas. Eula is on Farm Road 603 some seven miles southwest of Clyde in western Callahan County. In 1990, its population was estimated at 125. In 2000 its population remained the same. Eula had one store, one café, and three churches. Although I loved my childhood, that town, and everyone in it, I made a pact with myself that after graduation I was out of there, no matter what it took. I knew there was more waiting for me out in the world, and I wanted to experience it and chase it down.

College was a huge step in that direction for me. No one in my family at that point had gone to college, and I wasn't one of those kids whose parents had a college fund sitting there with my name on it. All I had was the dream in my heart, passion, enthusiasm, will, and a WHY to make it happen. I worked hard and earned a few scholarships that at least got me in the door and accepted to a small university in west Texas, but I knew that wasn't enough to keep me there for long.

So, I tried out for the cheerleading team and earned another scholarship. Then, I tried out for the track team and earned another scholarship. I organized my schedule so that I would complete all of my classes in the morning before lunch so that I would have all afternoon to devote to training, practice, and work. I worked odd jobs wherever I could find them in order to have food and spending money. My coach hired me as the groundskeeper for the track. I picked up trash, cleaned and organized all the equipment, mowed, picked weeds, and trimmed the fields. Whatever it took. I also started mowing lawns with a fellow track friend on weekends in Amarillo and got a job as a waitress. I was a door to door cutlery sales person and worked in the campus bookstore. I was determined to make it happen, so I studied hard, trained hard, and worked hard.

Was I the best on the track team? Not by a long shot. My high school didn't even have a rubber track. All we had was a dirt oval with a concrete barrier around it, so the odds of me going to college with a track scholarship were about 1%. Not to mention, there were people on the track team from all over the world who were recruited to go to school there just to be on the track team and who had full scholarships.

Was I the best on the cheerleading team? Not even close! Did I mention that my high school didn't even have football or competitive cheer? The only experience I had was cheering at basketball games.

Was I the smartest person in my classes? Absolutely not.

I knew that I was at a disadvantage in all areas, and if I wanted to earn more scholarship money to be able to complete school, I had to make up the difference by focusing on what I COULD do and work harder than anyone else.

Do you want to know what happened with that type of attitude? I won the MVP award and was named captain of the cheerleading squad. In track, I competed in Nationals every year and also won the All-Conference MVP award. The day I won that I had competed in over nine events. I graduated college with a double major in business and kinesiology. I did it!

After graduation, I got a job as the health and wellness director at a YMCA and guess what—they had ZERO budget for me to really do anything and were on the verge of closing their doors. So I got creative, rolled up my sleeves, and got to work. My main goal was to work with what I had at first—and that was myself—so I began building relationships, pouring into people, and changing the atmosphere. Then, I rearranged the equipment so it made more sense, fixed the broken pieces, kept it clean and tidy, and started a personal training program. Once a little money started coming in, I recovered the benches one by one so they matched and were not crusty and torn. Then I used the personal discount I had at the Sherwin Williams paint store because my brother-in-law was a store manager and painted the entire gym area. I then had enough money to replace the carpet with rubber flooring, but couldn't afford the installment, so I gathered some of the Y members and had them help me roll it out and glue it down. I then saw a need for child care because many parents wouldn't become members because they had no one to watch their children. So, I converted an empty room into a child care space. I painted murals on the walls, asked for donations of toys and used some of our part-time staff to watch the kids so that the parents could get their workouts in. It took about five years, but with a lot of hard work, long hours, and creativity, the Y became a thriving community that people enjoyed and wanted to be a part of!

During that time at the Y, I got another dream in my heart. I decided to compete in bikini competitions in the fitness and bodybuilding industry. Here we go again! Long story short, I started at the bottom and worked my way to the top. I began my journey by earning a sponsorship with a major supplement company for which I traveled the world promoting their products. Then, I earned my pro status in bikini. And next, I was a nobody who worked my way to winning the fitness industry's most popular contest online, the Bodyspace Spokesmodel competition, and who started my own online personal training business. From there I got married, became a pro judge, and then traveled around the world judging the fittest bodies in the world.

My husband and I loved what we did, had many perks, and made a very good living doing it. We got to hang with fitness superstars and travel over 200,000 miles a year around the world "living the dream." It was fun and glamorous for a while, and then I began to see a different side of the sport and industry. I saw in many cases how blatant corruption, politics, drugs, sex, pornography, prostitution, alcohol, eating disorders, vanity, narcissism, and every kind of darkness revolved around the sport. It was dirty, and I won't get into the details here because that is not the purpose of this story. However, the worst part of all of it is that, in many instances, the industry leadership creates, allows, participates, encourages, and controls this culture.

Do you remember the quote that says, "You become like the five people you spend the most time with?" Well, one day I had this realization that I was now actually a part of this circle of destruction, and it was no longer okay with me. I looked at my life, what I was doing, who I was around, and it was not the type of person I wanted to become. It's scary how fast your life can change when you aren't focused on the right things. I wanted to inspire people and give them hope, not lead them down a path of destruction, despair, death, and heartache. So, after a lot of soul-searching, we stepped down from our position and birthed another dream and vision for our lives and the lives of those in this industry. We decided that if no one else would take the responsibility to really care for the people in this sport, then we would have to be the ones to stand up and do it.

I can't even describe to you the amount of pain we endured after the separation. That world can be very cultish, and they use fear to control people, so we began to get threats, our family members received threats, lies were spread, and friend after friend acted like they had never known us.

Because of the loss of our entire community and extreme financial devastation, my husband went through a very deep, dark depression that lasted almost three years. During that time he was having thoughts of suicide and major anxiety, so we barely left the house except on the weekends when we had events and had to act like everything was okay. It was a surreal, scary, and painful experience to say the least, but we had a job to do, and even though the very people that we were trying to help refused to see or couldn't see our vision, it didn't matter because we knew we had to keep going anyway. We also had little to no support from sponsors or vendors because they were also threatened not to do business with us. So, we had to get creative and figure out a way to make it work with no financial help whatsoever. God came in and totally wrecked our hearts and saved my husband. And once we realized that our purpose was bigger than our pain, we rolled up our sleeves and got busy!

We decided to take all that we had learned, both the good and the bad, and create a new culture in the bodybuilding and fitness industry founded on transparency, fairness, and equality. Our goal was to be a safe, positive, healthy, family-friendly environment that would celebrate the journey and help people live healthier without having to go to such extremes with dieting, drugs, and playing political charades.

To accomplish this we created new divisions such as body transformation, bikini beach, bikini athletic, men's physique beach, men's physique athletic, and men's physique classic along with figure, fitness, and women's physique which celebrate and embrace all body types at every age and allow athletes to reach their health and fitness goals by living and competing healthily. We invested in a tablet-based judging system that takes us leaps and bounds above all other federations and customized it to take politics and unfairness out of play. We mic our judges up, and they are the emcees for the event. They talk about the differences between categories and what they look for when judging. They are also separated so they can't discuss competitors off-mic and be swayed by each other's opinions. Then the scores are tabulated by an average of two rounds and are based on mathematical numbers. The athletes get more time on stage and receive instant feedback and critiques with a five-star rating system so that, after the event, they can log in and see what they need to work on to improve their scores for the next competition. We now have events in major cities all across the United States. We also have athletes who fly from other countries such as Brazil, Ukraine, Europe, and Asia to compete in our events because they appreciate, believe in, and love the positive culture we have built!

In sharing these stories with you, I hope you take with you these three keys to success:

1. **Start where you are.** If you keep waiting for success to be delivered to your front door on a silver platter, you will be waiting

forever. You must take ownership of your future, and you must start now, today, exactly where you are at this very moment. You don't have to move, you don't need a million dollars, and you don't need an agency or a team to start. All you need to start is YOU.

2. **Use what you've got.** Stop focusing on what you don't have and instead focus on the dream in your heart. Your dream is a picture of the future, and if you use that as a guidepost to know where you are going, you won't get stuck on where you are at now. Remember that passion and enthusiasm are free! Your passion determines success' timing. If you are passionate, enthusiastic, hustling, and putting all-out effort into it, then you will start meeting the right people and making the right connections, and success will begin chasing you down.

3. **Do what you can.** Pray, meditate on your goal, and focus. It doesn't cost you anything to stay positive, but it does take effort and focus. What are you telling yourself? Negative thoughts are like a bucket of water dousing the fire of your dreams. Your input determines your output. Control the conversation inside your mind. Don't let it control you. Make sure you are feeding yourself positivity for breakfast, lunch, and dinner. Don't stop trying. Where there is a WHY, there is a WAY. Effort is free, but worry, quitting, and regret will cost you everything. Regret looks back, worry looks around, but victory looks up. The one trait that successful people have is that they keep going when others give up.

Do what you can, with what you've got, where you are at.

TWEETABLE
Don't stop trying. Where there is a WHY, there is a WAY. The one trait that successful people have is that they keep going when others give up.

Jennifer Thompson is a successful influencer (two million plus followers on social media), entrepreneur, lifetime natural athlete, bikini pro, certified personal trainer, weight-loss coach, and CEO & Co-Founder of the Nspire Sports League - NSL.

Because she has overcame the odds to find success, her passion for helping others do the same is her driving force. She loves seeing her clients grow and accomplish things they never imagined were possible. Where there is a WHY, there is a way!

Connect with Jennifer for training and to learn more about the NSL community:

jenthompsonfitness.com

NspireSL.com

IG: @jen_thompsonfit

FB: @jenthompsonfitness

SNAP: @jenjenyall

EMAIL: jenthompsonfit@gmail.com

CHAPTER 37

Your Enlightened Self-Interest

by Robert Helms

"When the why becomes clear, the how becomes obvious."
– Jim Rohn

C an you really make a living doing what you love? And if so, do you honestly know what you'd love to do if you could make a living at it? What is your life's work? Your compelling why? Your major definite purpose?

These are not easy questions. But they are worth really pondering if you want to see extraordinary results in your life.

I like to joke that I had a job once…and it was the worst two weeks of my life! The act of going to work doing something you don't enjoy for someone you don't care about just to make money has always felt wrong to me. Sure we all need to make a living, but the folks in my life that seem to be the happiest (and often the wealthiest) are doing something that matters to them.

For some, passion comes easy. Others need to search before discovering what they are passionate about.

One of my passions is real estate. Growing up I loved to play monopoly, and as I got older I watched my dad (an investor in seven different decades—we call him the "Godfather of Real Estate") acquire properties and cash flow, and I saw that monopoly wasn't just a board game. It was something I could do in real life. Once I figured that out, I was on a mission to not only build my portfolio, but also to spread the word. My first outlet for that was as a real estate salesperson, and later I continued by by educating people about real estate investing.

Most folks know me as the host of The Real Estate Guys™, a radio talk show on real estate investing that has been broadcasting on traditional radio since 1997 and is one of the top downloaded podcasts on real estate. A big part of my passion for helping folks discover the many benefits associated with the vehicle of real estate is fulfilled through sharing ideas and amazing guests on the show and producing live events that help people build wealth through real estate investing of all kinds.

On the show, we rarely talk about our "day" jobs. And while I used to sell real estate for a living, for more than 15 years I've expressed my passion for property through development.

As an international real estate development company, one of the things we always do is find ways to benefit the communities we serve. Since we don't work in our own backyard, we strive to not only make a profit, but also to create meaningful work for talented people. And...this may sound crazy... we overpay them.

If you own a business, you understand how costly turnover can be. By paying more than most, we attract great people who tend to stay longer. Jim Rohn called it "enlightened self-interest." Self-interest would be trying to get by paying as little as possible without them quitting. Paying them more—so that they'll stay and contribute—is the enlightened part.

We don't stop there.

As our business grows, rather than just hiring more people, we look for ways to keep them engaged and show them opportunity. So we suggest...in fact, we encourage team members who excel to consider starting their own business as a subcontractor.

We first came to Belize in 2004 as we were searching for another market that would allow us and our investors to diversify offshore. When we saw the labor landscape, we set a goal to help launch 50 new businesses in the country, which in turn would create new jobs, additional revenue, and more business for local vendors. A few of these companies would be our own, but the majority would belong to local people who started with us as employees and then could see the opportunity to work on their own. At last count, we have incubated more than 20 businesses, and we show no sign of stopping. And, in spite of spinning off business owners, we remain in the top five private employers in Belize.

How did that happen?

Clarity. We got clear on what we wanted and how we wanted to get there. In Belize, labor is inexpensive. For that reason, many companies find it easier to just hire more people than to spend time, energy, and money training the ones they have. And frankly, most construction jobs are short-lived. An unskilled laborer might get a job for 4 to 10 weeks, then go another 4 to 10 weeks before finding another one. A skilled craftsman might fare better, but not by much.

We took a different approach.

In our first year of operations, with around 40 employees, we invited them all to participate in an optional program of financial education. We held a weekly book study on *Rich Dad Poor Dad* by Robert Kiyosaki. Now, there's a very good chance you've read that book, but the same cannot be said for Belizeans. None of them knew anything about the book or how it could help them. So we explained our intentions to help them to better understand their finances so they would be able to accumulate wealth over time.

We made them pay for the books, though not full price, as the Rich Dad Company made the books available to us at wholesale. What's more, as a personal favor, Robert was kind enough to sign each one. Now that was a cool surprise that didn't mean much to our book study members at the beginning, but eventually, it would.

18 signed up for the book study, and 16 showed up to the first meeting. I handed out the books then explained who Robert Kiyosaki was and how popular the book was all over the world and then told them that Robert had signed the books for them.

One man asked how many of these books had been sold. I told him I wasn't sure, but well over 20 million at that time. He then asked how many of those had be signed by the author. Again, I wasn't sure, but guessed maybe ten thousand.

"Are these more valuable because they're signed?" he asked.

I replied, "Well, yes, they probably are."

"So then," he continued "can I sell this one and make some money?"

Everyone laughed, and I suggested "You can, but why don't you read it first, then sell it, then order a new one and ask Robert to sign it when he comes here next time?"

We spent the next hour talking about finances, how the rich don't work for money, and the difference between an asset and a liability. They were extremely interested, and it was as though they were learning a new language.

One of the workers was named Rudy, but his nickname on the jobsite was "Bonehead." He had one of the hardest jobs in the project, but he explained that everyone called him that because he wasn't very smart. But as we were closing the meeting, Rudy raised his hand.

"Yes, Rudy?" I said.

"Mr. Robert, it sounds like if I spend less money on sodas at work and girls on the weekend, then I'll have more money to invest in things that put money into my pocket instead of take it away."

All I could say was "Class dismissed." Rudy wasn't stupid. He just lacked mentors.

After class, I told Rudy, "It's time for your nickname to be changed from 'Bonehead' to 'Super Rudy.'"

We are in business to make a profit. But we do that by investing in our team and showing them the path to a brighter future.

So, what does this mean to you? Hopefully you've gotten some ideas about how to create a business that makes money and also does something important for the people who come to work every day to make that money. There is no set formula. You figure it out as you go.

This book is full of amazing stories of people who have pursued their dreams and found their purpose in business and even in life. But don't just read the stories. Be sure to find a lesson or two from each one that you can apply to your life.

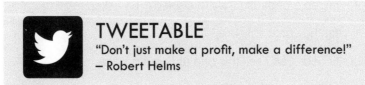

TWEETABLE
"Don't just make a profit, make a difference!"
— Robert Helms

Robert Helms is a professional real estate investor with experience in nine states and six countries. As a former top-producing real estate agent, Robert ranked in the top 1% of sales in the world's largest real estate organization. Robert's investment and development companies have projects valued at over $800 million. He is the co-author of Equity Happens – Building Lifelong Wealth with Real Estate *and the host of the nationally syndicated radio show* The Real Estate Guys™, *now in its twenty-first year of broadcast. The podcast version of the show is one of the most downloaded podcasts on real estate and is heard in more than 190 countries.*

https://realestateguysradio.com

WHAT OTHERS ARE SAYING

"Kyle, Friendship is wealth and you make me a rich man. Thanks for being a friend and partner all these years. Love and Respect!"

— **Jim Rohn (1930-2009), America's Foremost Business Philsopher**

"Kyle is simply a marketing genius! Every marketing dilemma I have ever had, Kyle has given me the brilliant and elegant solution on the spot. His consulting has saved and earned me hundreds of thousands of dollars over the years."

— **Darren Hardy, Former Publisher *SUCCESS* Magazine**

"I have worked closely with Kyle Wilson for 25 years. He is one of the best all-around marketers, promoters, business-builders and entrepreneurs in the business today. We have generated more than a million dollars together."

— **Brian Tracy, Author of *The Psychology of Achievement***

"Kyle Wilson single handedly changed the way I look at life! And the way I participate in my own! His wisdom, loyalty and commitment to seeing people soar is unmatched in the industry. He is a spring board, sounding board and ultimately, a launch pad for anyone committed to pursuing their deepest dreams and ultimate goals! He is the most authentic mentor, friend and business parter I've ever had."

— **Erika De La Cruz, TV & Media Host, Speaker, Trainer and Author of *Passionistas***

"Kyle is one of my old and dear friends and one of the smartest marketing guys I have had the opportunity to work with. He is the scrappy marketing guy. What I mean by that is, there are lots of guys who will put out business plans and do all kinds of nonsense and swing for home runs. Kyle is the real deal and finds ways to create product, add value, help people, build community, he's unbelievable."

— **Eric Worre, Founder of Network Marketing Pro and International Best-Selling Author of *Go Pro – 7 Steps to Becoming a Network Marketing Professional***

"If wanting to break into the speaker, author, marketing world, no one knows and does it better than my 10 year friend, Kyle Wilson. He is responsible for millions of people having access to the brilliant wisdom of Jim Rohn and so many other business thought leaders. He attracts the best people to his Inner Circle, something I'm proud to be a part of. I'm also excited to be working on a new book with Kyle, Lessons From Sports. Honored by his friendship."

— **Newy Scruggs, 7x Emmy-Winning Broadcaster**

"Kyle Wilson is not only one of my most valued friends and mentors, he is a marketing genius and brilliant business man always providing the most honest and insightful solutions to any challenge. I am honored to have him as my book partner and life long counterpart."

— Jeanette Ortega, Best-Selling Author of *The Little Black Book of Fitness* & Celebrity Fitness Trainer

"Kyle is one of the wisest and most brilliant marketing consultants in the world. He is the man behind the great marketing of Jim Rohn and so many other personal development legends. He is not only someone I've enjoyed collaborating and working with for over two decades, but also a close and valued friend. I recommend Kyle without equivocation."

— Mark Victor Hansen, Co-Creator of *Chicken Soup for the Soul*

"Kyle Wilson's Inner Circle Masterminds have been some of the most enlightening events I've been a part of the past few years. I've met so many incredible people outside the world I live and work in. It is the pinnacle of places you can go to upgrade your network. Kyle and this group is one I'm proud to associate with."

— Seth Mosley, 2x Grammy Winner, Billboard #1 Producer and Song Writer of the Year

"Kyle Wilson is the best marketer I know. In the 20 years I have known him, everything he touches and every idea he generates turns into money. If you're looking for a degree of fame and a higher degree of wealth, I recommend you connect with Kyle as fast as you can."

— Jeffrey Gitomer, Author of *The Little Red Book of Selling*

"Over the last 25 years, we've done several things together. Kyle is the only guy who has always under-promised and over-delivered on anything we have done together."

— Tom Ziglar, CEO of Ziglar, Inc.

"Kyle Wilson's insight, marketing acumen and business knowledge are guru level. His consulting, friendship and brilliant solutions have changed the trajectory of my career and life. His strategies don't just elevate, they transform you and your brand. "

— Olenka Cullinan, Speaker, Passionista, Founder of Rising Tycoons & #iStartFirst Bossbabe Bootcamps

"Kyle is a valued friend, a marketing superstar and one of the most knowledgeable people in the personal development industry."
— **Robin Sharma, Best-Selling Author of *The Monk Who Sold His Ferrari***

"Kyle, you ROCKED the EOFIRE show. You are a great story teller and shared great lessons. Truly impressed… and thank you for what you do/have done for this Entrepreneurial world."
– **John Lee Dumas, Host of EOFire Podcast with over 100 million downloads**

"Kyle Wilson is my 20 year plus valued friend and business/marketing coach. He is one of the most influential and connected people around. Kyle ALWAYS brings value to every relationship he is a part of."
– **Robert Helms, Real Estate Developer and Host of the #1 Podcast *The Real Estate Guys Radio Show***

"I met Kyle Wilson 12 years ago. It was almost magical how Kyle helped me in less than 12 months sell more products, pay off massive debt and booked me to speak all over the world with some of the biggest names in the speaking business. I can't strongly recommend his wisdom, knowledge, business mind or who he is as a person enough."
– **Ron White, Best-Selling Author of Black Belt Memory, 2009 & 2010 US Memory Champion**

"Kyle took me to 60 speaking engagements a year while increasing my fee, and helped me publish numerous books that sold nearly a million copies, taught me how to sell product from the back of a room and got me my own television show and a co-host with Zig Ziglar. There is not a single person alive who not only knows but has mastered the speaking business from beginning to end like Kyle Wilson."
– **Chris Widener, Bestselling Author *The Angel Inside***

"Kyle Wilson is the man! When I made the decision to transition from my 15 year MLB career to being a speaker, best-selling author and business consultant I researched and then sought out the man who has been behind such iconic speakers as Jim Rohn, Brian Tracy and many others. Hiring Kyle as my coach has been one of the smartest decisions I made."
– **Todd Stottlemyre, Author of *Relentless Success*, 15 year MLB pitcher and 3x World Champion**

GET CONNECTED

To Learn More About the
Kyle Wilson Inner Circle Mastermind

Go to KyleWilsonMastermind.com
or send an email to info@kylewilson.com
with *Inner Circle* in the Subject.

For details on upcoming events

Go to KyleWilsonEvents.com

Receive Your Special Bonuses for Buying
***Purpose, Passion & Profit* Book**

Send an Email to
gifts@PurposePassionProfitBook.com